THE JURY

HAS A VERDICT!

A TED BORN

COURTROOM DRAMA

First Printing 2022

ISBN Paperback 978-1-7357825-8-4

ISBN Hardback 978-1-7357825-9-1

TABLE OF CONTENTS

PREFACE

The Jury Has a Verdict! is the third of a trilogy of legal Courtroom dramas/thrillers featuring fictitious attorney Ted Born, and it is a prequel to the first two: *The Impossible Mock Orange Trial* and *The Vow: Ted Born's Last Trial.* While denominated as Courtroom dramas/thrillers, all three of the books narrate the struggles of an ethical lawyer trying to achieve his conception of justice for his clients, often in the face of heavy odds against him. In his efforts he of course must deal with opposing counsel and opposing parties, juries, and Judges. The present work focuses on Ted Born's interactions with Judges and juries, exploring several different experiences as he strives to achieve justice for his clients. Ultimately, the reader must ponder the question, *What is justice?*, as the narratives lay out the competing ways of viewing the facts of each case.

Society is sustained by its institutions, accepted, or at

least not actively opposed, by the people at large. Those who hold positions of authority in the administration of the institutions, such as Judges, may, from time to time, fall short of their duties or the public's expectations of those duties, either by failings of character or judgment, and yet the institutions survive, and society moves forward, perhaps making course corrections along the way. That is why we often say that the offices held by officials deserve our respect and deference even when there are misgivings about specific actions of the officials themselves.

The judiciary is among the most vital of our institutions, as it is this body that resolves disputes and differences among persons or segments of society, a lid with pressure valves that can at least moderate the overheated caldron of rancor and embedded anger that otherwise might explode into violence or even revolution. Because we have a considerable degree of respect for the institution of the judiciary as an interpreter of the law and of our rights and obligations, we generally accept the ultimate rulings of Judges, even when we disagree with particular decisions, and even when we feel that our concepts of "justice" have not been satisfied.

Judges are selected generally by appointment or by election, and some of the appointments, such as Federal Judges, are for life tenure, subject to good behavior and the consequent possibility of impeachment. Others are elected or appointed for specific terms of service. Judges almost always come from the body of society's lawyers, and they enter onto their judicial duties bearing all of the influences that have accumulated from childhood, honed by their experiences at the legal bar. That is to say, they bring with them a body of academic learning in law and culture, tempered by their convictions, biases, moral compasses, likes and dislikes, and physical, mental and emotional conditions that all human beings have. Oliver Wendell Holmes, in his famous *The Path of the Law* lecture, said:

> The language of judicial decision is mainly the language of logic. And the logical method and form flatter that longing for certainty and for repose which is in every human mind. But certainty generally is illusion, and repose is not the destiny of man. Behind the logical form lies a judgment as to the relative worth and importance of competing legislative grounds, often an inarticulate and unconscious judgment, it is true, and yet the very root and nerve of the whole proceeding.

Judges are thrust into an environment where they are expected to be fair and impartial, constrained by the statutory law and precedents which presumably bind them, and also by the verdicts of jurors who decide the facts to which the law is to be applied. Yet, within those constraints, Judges have enormous leeway and power, including the timing of hearings and trials, rulings on sometimes critical pretrial motions, granting or denying temporary restraining orders and preliminary injunctions, rulings on evidentiary issues, and even setting aside, in whole or in part, jury verdicts when it is felt the verdicts are not supported by the evidence.

The lawyers who represent litigants in Court must interact with Judges in numerous ways and on numerous occasions over the course of litigations. In their pursuit of justice for their clients, lawyers have a strong incentive to maintain relations with Judges which are at least neutral and preferably confidence-inspiring and cordial, while carefully maintaining a respectful wall of separation and deference between bench and bar. On the one hand, a lawyer is an officer of the Court, bound to respect Judges, accept their ultimate judgments, and bound to promote respect for the Judges among clients and the public. Yet, while a lawyer has strong obligations to the Court and its Judges, he or she also has strong fiduciary duties to represent clients' causes as effectively as possible within the limits of propriety. There may be times in the career of a lawyer when he or she believes a certain trial Judge is in error, to the client's detriment, and reluctantly sees no alternative but to take measures in the client's interest that, despite taken respectfully and politely, nevertheless irritate the Judge and engender resentment. The lawyer thus can be caught in a quandary where there seem to be no good options whereby the duties to the Court and to the Client can both be perfectly accommodated.

This work includes one particularly traumatic situation where Ted Born appears to incur the wrath of a

Federal Judge, while exerting every effort to avoid it. The reader should feel the exhilaration of Ted Born at moments of triumph, as well as his agony when he finds himself on the wrong side of a Federal Judge. While it is the author's intent to provide an entertaining and engaging legal Courtroom drama, the ultimate motif is an exploration of how fragile the pursuit of justice can be in the context of a legal system that is the best in the world but presents real life challenges as well.

Judges do not always get it right, however hard they try, but judicial review is the safeguard built into our institutions that aids the cause of justice.

In a jury trial, once a case advances beyond the intervention of the Judge, the fate of the parties is largely in the hands of the jury, a group of citizens about whom the parties and the lawyers have limited information. While there are tools and purported wisdom for striking potential jurors to produce an impartial jury, lawyers generally know relatively little about those chosen for jury service and cannot be sure how they may react to the evidence presented. One of the tensest of moments for lawyers, when their hearts skip a few beats and they struggle for breath and composure, is when the bailiff comes to them and says, "The jury has a verdict. Please return to the Courtroom." At that point, the lawyers have done all they can do; they can only watch and listen as the foreperson of the jury hands up the jury form to the Judge. It can be a moment of celebration or despair.

The cases in this book are fictitious and neither the persons, living or dead, nor the events are intended to portray any actual persons or events, although they are inspired by various actual experiences of the author in his practice of law.

CHAPTER ONE

NEVER GET ON THE WRONG SIDE OF A JUDGE

Ted Born and his young associate Jamie Fletcher were driving back from a trial – Jamie's very first trial, talking to each other about the experience as they returned home from the out-of-town trial. Their client, Lumber Products Inc., was a lumber-grading company that trained and licensed employees of lumberyards how to evaluate and certify the correct grade of each piece of lumber at their lumberyard, using a scale of 1 to 5, with number 1 being the highest grade. They would stamp their certification on each piece with the grade of the lumber and the certification logo of Lumber Products, somewhat like a brand name, that assured customers they could rely on the specified quality of that lumber.

The defendant was a lumberyard named Balentine Lumber, that had not been licensed by Lumber Products to use its logo on any Ballentine lumber; they had once had that right, but they abused it by a combination of deliberate and careless marking, so Lumber Products had yanked their right to use its logo, an action also taken by the other major grade-marking agency, for the same reason. So, Balentine had no right to use any recognized certification logo for its lumber, making it very difficult to sell significant quantities of lumber, as contractors would not buy uncertified lumber.

An opportunity came up for Balentine to sell a large quantity of lumber at a very good price, but only if it was No. 1 grade and only if the lumber was logo certified. Balentine's solution was to bribe a lumberyard that had a legitimate authorized logo stamp to lend the stamp to Balentine for marking its lumber, the key to making the big sale. The guy who brought the stamp over to Balentine was wined and dined and furnished with female company overnight, while the Balentine employees used the borrowed stamp to mark almost every piece of lumber in the yard No. 1 grade. There was a full moon that night illuminating the lumberyard, and they took advantage of that natural light, supplemented by a few flashlights, to accomplish their mission. The next morning the vis-iting stamp bearer retrieved his stamp and went home with sealed lips and a pocketful of money. Of course, the lumber was so badly off-grade that the defects were readily detectible and traced back to Balentine. Lumber

Products hired Ted Born to get an injunction and recover damages from Balentine. But Balentine, though guilty as sin, was surprisingly resistant to a proper settlement, so Ted had to sue.

Jamie said, "You commissioned me to find an expert witness who could testify about damages our client had sustained, mainly damage to the value of the reputation and good name of our client's imprimatur associated with reliable grade marks. Problem was, we had our own doubts as to whether his calculations would hold up on appeal. Calculating damages to goodwill is a devilishly difficult thing to do, at least in the wholesale lumber business. Thank goodness we got a real good jury verdict in our favor, but the jury designated the entire recovery as *compensatory* damages, and we had been hoping they would classify most of it as *punitive* damages, as a penalty for intentional wrongdoing. How do we deal with that now, Ted? Won't Ballentine file post-trial motions to set aside the jury verdict, contending there was inadequate proof of compensatory damages?"

"I feel sure they will," said Ted. "There would have been no problem if the jury had just denominated the figures as punitive damages, because the intentional egregious nature of the conduct certainly warranted that. The jury apparently felt our client deserved the dollars they awarded but they weren't aware of the problem they created when they dumped it all into the compensatory bucket, where we have a much tougher job to defend it, just because it is so difficult to quantify with hard evidence the magnitude of injury to goodwill. There is a doctrine, though, that says: when the *fact* of damages is certain, but the quantification is inherently uncertain, the plaintiff - us – is allowed to make a good faith effort to calculate the damages, and then the burden shifts to the defendant to *disprove* it. That doctrine could save us. Let's research this carefully and get ready to do our best to defend the verdict."

Jamie chuckled, "Yeah, you know what sticks in my memory from the trial is, when you would ask Roger Balentine almost any question while he was testifying, his standard answer was either, 'I don't know,' or 'I don't remember.' And then you asked him, 'How many times in the past have you done this very same thing and didn't get caught?' and his answer was, 'I don't remember.' You really made hay out of that in your closing argument when you said, 'I just want you, the jury, to think about what Mr. Balentine said when I asked him how many times in the past had he done the same thing and hadn't got caught, and he said he couldn't remember.' You said, 'Mr. Balentine has done this so many times in the past to other people that he can't even remember how many times.' I saw some jurors nodding their heads at that one. And then you cautioned our client not to show much emotion regardless how the verdict came out, and he didn't; but he pointed at me and told you that you had warned the wrong person! I've got to admit, being my first jury trial, I just could not contain myself when we got that verdict. Novice excitement, I guess," Jamie grinned.

Balentine Lumber did indeed file post-trial motions, in the process replacing its trial lawyer and getting themselves some new lawyers to handle their motions for a new trial and for judgment notwithstanding the verdict. They made the predictable arguments in their briefs to set aside the jury verdict, for lack of reliable proof of actual damages. Ted and Jamie countered in their reply brief with the doctrine Ted had proffered, but they were nervous about the outcome. Ted knew Judge Newton grew up in or near the town where the Balentine lumberyard was and probably knew their reputation for shady dealing, and certainly their conduct in this particular case was totally in character with their bad reputation.

The hearing on the post-trial motions was held in Judge Newton's Chambers. Instead of dealing immediately with the merits of the motions, Judge Newton first brought up a different subject. He told the assembled lawyers he had received a telephone call from an old friend asking him to "go easy" on the Balentines. The Judge said he was so taken aback that, although he should have lectured the guy, instead he just made an excuse and quickly hung up the telephone – said the man had been very kind to his elderly mother, so he instinctively did not read him the riot act but just hung up the phone. He asked if either side wanted him to recuse himself, and both said 'no.' The Judge then proceeded to hear arguments on the post-trial motions, and he denied them. However, he urged the parties to discuss settlement before deciding whether to appeal.

When Ted and Jamie got back to their office, Ted said, "I'll always wonder how much effect the reputation of the Balentines influenced the Judge's decision. I mean, justice was certainly done, as I see it, and certainly the Balentine family's fraudulent actions should have inclined the Judge in our direction, coupled with their evasive conduct on the witness stand. But they had a bad reputation before all that, and I feel confident Judge Newton knew of it. I can't complain, because we came out fine, but I still wonder."

"Ted, are you saying the Judge should possibly have recused himself before the trial because he might have already had a negative impression of the Balentines?" Jamie asked.

"No, I'm not saying that," answered Ted. "Unless there had been personal dealings with the Balentines in the past, like a confrontation of some kind, I don't think knowledge of their reputation would require a recusal, assuming he believed he could be impartial. But justice is a complicated thing. You might say that justice is just applying the statutory law and precedents to the facts of a case, but statutes have to be interpreted, and precedents have nuances and ambiguities as well, to say nothing of the infinite variations of fact situations to which the law must be applied. And the application of the law to the facts is done by Judges who are not robots; they bring with them all of their life experiences, all the things they've been exposed to, and to some degree everything in their backgrounds will naturally affect their decisions. It might not be a decisive influence, or even a material influence, but, because they are human, there will probably be some sort of influence. Let's take an obvious example. Let's assume two lawyers argue a motion before a Judge. One of the lawyers has been practicing for many years, has a reputation for candor as well as good legal scholarship, is courteous, and has a record of winning cases. The other lawyer is young, perhaps a recent addition to the bar, and has no reputation one way or another for candor or legal scholarship. Which lawyer's arguments are going to enjoy the greatest attention and respect of the Judge? Obviously, a highly conscientious Judge will give equal attention and credence to both arguments. But it is hard to avoid the suspicion that experienced lawyers with a reputation for competence and candor will have an edge in terms of the Judge's receptivity. Again, it might not be decisive, but it is there, and it likely has some degree of influence."

"I'm a young and inexperienced lawyer," said Jamie. "The Judges don't know me. I'm going to do my best, but it's a little discouraging to think that my efforts might be less effective than an older and more experienced lawyer when we've both done our homework and are contesting the same point. What's your advice for me?"

"Remember, I said the difference might not be material or decisive. If you work hard, your reputation can build quickly, and scholarship counts for a whole lot. If logic and precedent are on your side, you have a good chance of winning, despite the receptivity premium enjoyed by some more senior lawyers. One more thing, NEVER, EVER, get on the wrong side of a Judge. If that happens, things get personal between you and the Judge, and human nature's tendency to disfavor a person you don't like, can be powerful and can overwhelm an awful lot of good things you might otherwise have going for you," Ted advised.

"I guess you have good relations with all the Judges, don't you? What if you feel you are right and the Judge is wrong, and you have to take a position that offends the Judge in order to represent your client faithfully? Then what?" Jamie asked.

"I really don't know, Jamie. I would do everything possible to avoid offense, but of course the ethical representation of the client would have to be paramount in that situation. Of course, I've had to appeal rulings I thought were incorrect, but I have tried to do it deferentially, and so far, I don't think it has made any bad dents in my relationships with Judges. But I guess that could happen," Ted answered. "Just remember, move heaven and earth not to get on the wrong side of a Judge, especially a life-tenured Federal Judge."

The case was settled for a modest discount to avoid an appeal, and the client still got fair monetary compensation plus the all-important permanent injunction to prevent recurrences.

CHAPTER TWO

MEETING THE GRAND JURIES

"OK, Ted. You said you wanted to talk with me about a new case you had that I could help with, *Pure Fision,* I think. What have you got?" asked Jamie Fletcher.

"Actually, I don't think you could call it a case – or cases, at least not yet. And I'm not sure it's fair to ask you to get involved, because it's criminal law, and I doubt if you've done any of that yet. But let me tell you about the situation and see whether you think you would like to join me. Am I right in assuming you haven't had much exposure to criminal law?" Ted Born asked.

"Yes, you are right. I took a course in criminal law in law school, but I have always been focused on civil law since I came to the Firm," replied Jamie.

"All right, let me tell you about it. You probably know we represent a bottler of spring water and energy drinks called 'Pure Fision' – a coined name that suggests 'pure' water with fizzy bubbles, but deliberately misspelled with only one 's' in 'Fision,' to make the trademark a little more distinctive. Their market is generally the Carolinas and Georgia, with some sales in Virginia. Well, it seems there was a company headquartered in Ohio with a broad distribution of competing drinks in various pockets of the eastern United States, and it got caught fixing prices in Ohio with a couple of bottled water and energy drink competitors in that area. They pled guilty to illegal price fixing under Section 1 of the Sherman Act, paid a big fine and consented to an injunction. However, there were some high-ranking officers of the company who very likely could have gone to jail for their price fixing. In order to keep them out of jail, the company, Genretta, made a deal with the Justice Department that Genretta would direct each of its sales offices in the United States to conduct an investigation of any price fixing in their areas relating to the bottled drinks, and would report the results of those investigations to the Antitrust Division of the Justice Department."

"Sounds like a hornets' nest got activated," Jamie surmised.

"I'll say!" said Ted. "Apparently, as those investigative

reports have been reaching Justice, the Department has ordered its local field offices to check out the evidence of price fixing, and they're convening grand juries around the country to hear testimony. Where warranted, they are moving to get indictments against Genretta's co-conspirators – and it looks like the Department thinks it usually *is* warranted in most areas. Of course, Genretta and its employees don't get indicted in any of these new cases, as a reward for Genretta's cooperation. There have already been a bunch of criminal cases spawned all over the East that came about from Genretta's internal investigations that got turned over to Justice. One company resisted and went to trial, resulting in a massive defeat for the company, and some individuals got jail sentences. After that, it seems that almost every company accused of being a part of price fixing with Genretta has pleaded guilty and has swallowed its medicine.

"That brings me to our client, Pure Fision," Ted continued. "Our client competes in about four geographic areas with Genretta, and it has begun receiving subpoenas to produce documents to the grand juries and, later, to provide witnesses to testify before the grand juries. I have personally been meeting with our client's staff and salespersons, and thus far they adamantly deny any price fixing or anything that might be circumstantial evidence of price fixing. What they're telling me seems credible, because the prices in the areas where we compete with Genretta seem to be very low, and profit margins are also very thin. In addition, I've reviewed the documents requested by the grand juries, and they seem innocuous. We are now at the stage where witnesses are being called to testify. That's where I could use some help."

"Glad to help, Ted, but what do I do? Do I go to the grand jury hearings and object to leading or improper questions?" Jamie asked.

"No, unfortunately, you don't get to attend the grand jury hearing while your clients are being interrogated. For people - including lawyers – who aren't familiar with criminal law practice, it comes as a shock that a client doesn't get the benefit of counsel in a grand jury pro-ceeding, even though they could be asked incriminating questions. You may think, isn't that what a lawyer is for, to protect the client in legal proceedings? But that's not the way it works in grand jury hearings," Ted said with a tutorial smile.

"Well, what's the lawyer's role, then? What can we do to protect clients?" Jamie asked.

"There are some things we can do," Ted replied. "First, when you get a witness subpoena, the first thing you do is to talk with the Justice Department lawyer. You try to find out whether the witnesses being called are 'targets' of the investigation or are merely background witnesses. Sometimes, Justice won't tell you, and even when it does, you can't totally depend on it, because they can always claim that the witness did not become a target until lat-er. Certainly, if the witness really is just a background witness and not considered a likely target for indictment, most JD lawyers will be willing to grant immunity, either statutory immunity or informal 'letter immunity,' which just says the Government won't prosecute under certain conditions. However, letter immunity, although not as strong as statutory immunity, will essentially prevent the witness from being indicted, because it would likely be considered 'entrapment' if the witness relied on a promise of immunity, and then, after giving testimony, ended up being indicted anyway.

"But, note: this won't prevent the Government from prosecuting for perjury, if it can prove the witness was not truthful on the witness stand. The Government might want a preview of what the witness would say to the grand jury, and sometimes the prosecution might even tell you what it will be asking the witness. In the background of all of this is the Constitutional right not to self-incriminate. If the Government will not grant immunity, then the defense lawyer should carefully consider invoking the right against self-incrimination. In that case, if the defense lawyer cannot get reasonable immunity and the Justice Department insists that the witness appear and assert the right against self-incrimination, the lawyer should write out a statement for the witness to read, with the instruction to say nothing beyond his name, age, address, and employment - just reading the pre-prepared statement for everything else. Remember, only human beings have the right not to self-incriminate; corporations don't have that protection. It's really a pretty delicate dance you go through."

"Wow! I never learned this stuff in law school," Jamie exclaimed. "What else can a lawyer do to protect a client who's called as a witness?"

"You debrief him or her thoroughly and go over the anticipated testimony and be sure the witness is prepared for all the possible questions or tactics that might occur. You also accompany the witness to the site of the grand jury room and wait outside while the testimony takes place. If the witness feels that he or she is being harassed or browbeaten, or even if the questions take an unexpected turn that produce a level of unease or uncertainty, the witness can ask for a break to consult the lawyer waiting outside. Often, such a request will be accommodated if it is not used repetitiously or abusively. You understand what motivates the Justice Department, don't you? They don't care about the small fry and therefore they will grant immunity to them, hoping the little guys will testify against the big guys who are the ones the Department really wants to get, to make an example of them, by sending them to jail. It has a real deterrent effect, the Government thinks, when the newspapers print that some big shot, who was maybe a pillar of the community, has gone to jail for price fixing. Other executives begin to get nervous when they hear about that."

"So, what can I do to help, besides drinking a lot of bottled water and energy drinks while I'm waiting outside the grand jury room?" Jamie grinned.

"I have a case over in Columbia, where the grand jury is hearing witnesses. You know, the grand jury is 'grand,' I guess, because it has 23 members, not 12 or less, like the normal petit jury we usually think about. Theoretically, once the grand jury is impaneled, it can be a roving investigator and set its own agenda. But that rarely happens in antitrust cases. The Government lawyer is in the jury room with the jurors and he or she almost always decides what will be investigated and what witnesses will be called. The members of the grand jury can ask questions on their own, though the Government lawyer asks most of them, usually almost all of them. The grand jury will sit for a day or two, and then they may be sent home, to be called back for another day or two, sent home again, and then eventually they will vote on whether to indict. It takes only a majority of the grand jury to hand down an indictment - not required to be unanimous.

"There is a court reporter present who takes down all the testimony, but we won't see or hear any of it because the grand jury proceedings are secret, and everyone present is directed, and pledges, not to disclose any of the proceedings except that the witnesses - witnesses only - can tell all about their testimony and experience. Of course, if there is an indictment and we have to face trial, at that point the Government is required to turn over the grand jury transcripts of all the witnesses who are expected to testify at trial. In the meantime, you are sitting outside the grand jury room where your client or your client's employees are testifying, and there's not a lot you can do, unless there is evidence of abusive behavior by the prosecutors that you learn about during a break in the testimony. Mind you, there's no Judge sitting at a bench in the grand jury room, but in case of prosecutorial misconduct, you can go to a Judge and the Judge can exercise oversight over that kind of thing."

"What about documents, Ted? What if the prosecutors pull out some strange document the witness has never seen and uses it to ambush the witness?" Jamie asked.

"Well, we will have already produced to the Government all documents responsive to their subpoena that are in our possession. The Government lawyers almost never call live witnesses until they have gotten all the documents that they think they need, so we will know about our documents and will have gone over them with the witness. If it's a surprise document that came out of the files of a competitor, the normal answer would be, 'I don't know anything about this; I did not write it or receive it.' Of course, if the surprise document implicates the witness in some sort of wrongdoing that the witness thinks is incorrect, the answer would be, 'That never happened,' or 'it happened an entirely different way,' assuming such is true. We will have chances after the testimony to look into that and develop evidence about it. Right now, we have already produced our documents to the Government counsel, and we are at the live testimony phase," Ted explained.

"Do you see any problems in the documents we've produced?" Jamie asked.

"Not a thing, Jamie," Ted answered. "And looking at the landscape from 200 feet above, I don't see anything, either. Prices are low in our markets, compared with other markets, and the water bottlers and energy drink bottlers are competing against the major soft drink bottlers to some extent, as thirsty customers can choose from soft drinks, bottled water or energy drinks, and there could be no effective conspiracy unless the major bottlers joined in. I see no evidence of that, nor does the Government seem to be contending there was participation of the majors. It's all a mystery to me. Of course, if there was a price-fixing conspiracy, even between two insignificant players in the market, that would be illegal, and a *per se* criminal violation of the antitrust laws, but it would be futile without participation by the majors. Can't figure out what's behind all this. Doesn't make sense."

"Maybe they have some evidence we don't know about. Every conviction they get is another notch in their guns, another item on a Department lawyer's résumé, aiding his or her career advancement. At last count, you mentioned the Justice Department had a perfect record of convictions or guilty pleas in this set of cases. I can see it's intimidating, to say the least," Jamie observed. "I will get with our witnesses for the Columbia grand jury, and I will probe hard to see what they know, prepare them for what they can expect, and then be sure I have something to sit on outside the grand jury room when they testify."

The next week Jamie found himself in the basement of the Federal Courthouse in Columbia. Ted had told him most grand juries seem to meet in dank basement rooms in the Federal Courthouses, often in the vicinity of a concessions stand where usually disabled veterans are employed to sell crackers, coffee, and soft drinks. There was bottled water, but it did not bear the "Pure Fision" label. It turned out to be an uncontentious event and did not last long. The two witnesses, a man and a woman, were salespeople. They reported that they were asked whether they knew the salespeople of other bottlers, especially those of Genretta, and they said they knew the Genretta crew mainly by reputation. They were asked whether they had ever met with them or talked by telephone with their competitors. The Pure Fision witnesses testified they did not believe they had ever been in a meeting with them, or talked with them by telephone, unless you count attending a soft drink bottling association annual meeting with lots of employees working in the industry. Had they ever discussed pricing with their competitors? Absolutely not, they testified. They were shown no documents other than some price lists put out by the various competitors. They testified they had never coordinated any price announcements with competitors, and there seemed no price sheets approximately simultaneously dated, although the prices themselves were close or identical, as one would expect in the case of commodity products.

Jamie made notes of his debriefing conference
with the witnesses. Back at the office, he reported the
apparent non-event to Ted Born. Ted and Jamie were
puzzled at the whole thing. A few weeks later, the
Justice Department lawyers notified Ted that they were
dismiss-ing the grand jury in Columbia and in two other
locations without any action against Pure Fision.
There was one remaining investigation that was still
open, in Savannah.

CHAPTER THREE

THE SAVANNAH ENIGMA

"What do you know about Savannah, Jamie?" Ted Born asked Jamie Fletcher, sitting on the other side of Ted's desk.

Jamie looked puzzled, "Not a whole lot, Ted. Although I'm a Georgia kid originally, from north Georgia, I never had relatives in Savannah or any special reasons to go there. But I've been to Savannah a few times – real nice town; I like it a lot, reminds me of Charleston. Why do you ask? Must be something cooking there besides the Brunswick stew."

"Could be, Jamie. It's the one place in Pure Fision's market area where the Justice Department is still apparently trying to make something out of a suspected price-fixing conspiracy. I've had a call from the company President, Burton Teague, and his company has just received a subpoena for in-person testimony of the Savannah Sales Manager and one of the assistant managers. It could be just like the other ones, duds. But the Prez says this situation might not be as clear as the others. I've told him he should not discuss the case with the two witnesses and that the witnesses should not discuss the case with each other, or with anyone else in the office. We want them to testify as to what they really know, not what someone else has told them. But the Prez says he knows of no contacts or communications, about prices, between these fairly high-level officials and any employees of Genretta. He thinks any contacts have been on the up-and-up, no collusion, but we need to check it out. It involves Savannah, but some of the officials are here at the Greenville headquarters, so it will be easy for us to interview them first to see what they know. Others are stationed in Savannah, of course, and we'll have to go there as well. We need to check them out and get them immunity before they testify."

"OK. By the way, we just found out my wife is pregnant, first child. We're excited. It shouldn't interfere with my work, though," announced Jamie, beaming from ear to ear.

"Hey, that's great news, Jamie. Congratulations! You got married right out of law school, didn't you? I've met your wife at a few Firm functions. She's beautiful and seems extremely nice. You're a lucky man," Ted said, extending his hand for a congratulatory shake.

"Yeah, she's special, helped straighten me out, frankly. When I went to college, I was going to major in accounting. I was a walk-on for the Frosh football team, which I did for one season, wasn't much good at that and did not continue. I got involved in fraternity life, in a big way, and I really was majoring in Frat. I was pretty wild and no-good. My grades went to hell. Then, in my Junior year, I met Helen, and there was something different and special about her. What she saw in me is still a puzzlement to this day, but she was a good friend and supportive. With her encouragement, I changed my major to business administration, and my grades improved. I decided I wanted to go to law school, but my grades overall weren't good enough to get into a top tier school. So, I was lucky to get into a law school that I thought was pretty good but not considered top tier, and by golly, the law excited me, and I got good grades, made law review, and it looked like maybe I had a future. Meanwhile, Helen had transferred to a school in Charleston, where she was doing real well. We had kept in touch, seeing each other when we could. She was also getting more and more religious, not fanatical, but it wasn't a casual thing for her either. She got me to reconnect with my own Faith which had once been important to me, too, in years past, but I had let it slide to the point it just wasn't there for me anymore. I began thinking, 'You know, Jamie, I'm not sure you can make it without this woman at your side. Heck, I'm not sure you *want* to make it without her.' Long story short, she was willing to take a chance on me, provided I was willing to settle in the Palmetto State of South Carolina. So here I am, and I'm so happy about how everything has turned out, I feel like shouting about it. I'm glad the Firm has been willing to take me on. I love it here. Confessions of a first-year associate, I guess! Forgive me if I've gotten too personal," Jamie expounded.

"Jamie, thanks so much for sharing that. Sounds a little like *The Confessions of St. Augustine*, or maybe the confessions of half our lawyers. We all spent years of our youth searching, taking chances, testing the limits, and hopefully settling on a stable foundation for living our lives. They say you never really get to know other persons, not even members of your immediate family. You see them in a certain context, here in the law firm, for example, working mutually on legal matters, but you don't get to know the whole person - their thoughts and dreams and all that. We need to know each other, *really* know each other, a lot better. And I can see that the Firm owes a great debt of gratitude to Helen for getting you here, because you have the potential to be a real star. You are bright, perceptive, friendly. You communicate well, on paper and orally, and communication is such an important part of being a lawyer – the ability to relate to all sorts of people, clients, partners and associates, Judges, and jurors, as well as opposing counsel. You have the brains and the right 'touch.' So, we are just delighted to have you and Helen in the Firm family, and in a little while we will be privileged to welcome another Fletcher to the Firm family. Congratulations, again!

"Meanwhile," Born continued, "let's interview our witnesses and see what kind of exposure we have. And let's start tomorrow morning. I'll see if I can arrange that. I think I can, because I have impressed on the client that this is a priority matter, that we need almost instant availability with key witnesses. The client is fully on board with that."

The next morning, Ted and Jamie went to the Pure Fision headquarters office, saw some higher-level corporate executives in Greenville, then realized they really needed to meet with Savannah Sales Manager Slade Webb and his assistant Cranford Evins, who of course were in Savannah. "Now, look, gentlemen, we are here to help," Ted told them. "We are on your side. But we need your full cooperation, and sometimes we might seem to be making a nuisance of ourselves, but bear with us. There is a reason for everything we will be doing, and it is for your protection and benefit. This is probably the only time we will meet together with both of you, and we want to be sure you NEVER, EVER talk between yourselves or with anyone else in the organization about this Government investigation of the bottled water and energy drink market. Why? Because we are not just talking about money – as important as that is. We are talking about possible jail sentences for any individuals found guilty of price-fixing collusion, and you can imagine that is very serious to you personally, to your families, and to your company. I am not trying to scare you, and it might be that you have nothing to fear. But people involved in sales are likely to be the ones involved in price fixing, if anyone is, and so you would be prime targets if there are some underlying antitrust problems. We don't want you discussing anything about this investigation, or any of your past contacts with competitors, with anyone other than us attorneys, because, in the first place, the Government lawyers will be able to ask you about anything you've *heard* in the office, whether or not you were involved in it, and we don't want your knowledge of past events contaminated by something you've heard that you have no firsthand knowledge about. This is serious, and we want you to be very strict about it. If you have any information, or any questions, call Jamie or me and talk about it, because there is an attorney-client privilege that protects you when you provide information to a lawyer representing and advising you. One other thing: if we get to a point where we think either one of you has legal exposure on account of past actions you have taken or been involved in, we might well need to get you counsel separate from the two of us, because we are primarily lawyers for the company. As long as there is no conflict between the company's interests and your personal interests, we can represent you both, but we will have to look closely at that if the situation changes. Do you have any questions?" No one had any questions, so Ted and Slade Webb went into one conference room and Jamie and Cranford Evins went into another.

Ted began interviewing Slade Webb. "Slade, I'm sure you know that you need to be entirely truthful with me, because I can't help you if I don't know the facts – at least the facts as you see and remember them. The worst thing that could happen would be for you to hold back and let us get out on a limb, only to find out the Government's got evidence that makes you look like a liar. If you lose credibility, you lose everything. So, I need for you to tell me every single contact you have had with a competitor, whether in a personal meeting, a group meeting, a telephone call, smoke signals, or whatever. So let me hear from you. I assume you probably know, know of, or have met your counterparts at Genretta."

Webb looked at Born intently, frowned a little, and said, "Mr. Born, I'm not quite sure what to say, because I don't think there have been any contacts of the kind you're interested in, but I will tell you what I know. First, there was a bill in the Georgia Legislature to impose a sales tax on the sale of non-alcoholic bottled beverages. Of course, that got the attention of all the bottlers – us, Genretta, and the major soft drink bottlers. Someone, I think one of the soft drink bottlers, proposed we all chip in some money to fund our opposition to the tax. We contributed modestly to that fund, and we had a meeting or two, but nobody said anything whatsoever about pricing of any of our products."

Born broke in, "Let me interrupt you right there. Did anyone say something like, 'Prices are terrible, or competition is too intense.' Anything like that?"

"No, I've sure had that opinion, because our prices in Savannah *are* so low that I feel like I'm working in a charitable organization, but nobody said a word about it. Our focus was on defeating the proposed tax," Webb said convincingly.

"Well, it's not illegal for competitors to get together to oppose legislation. You have a Constitutional right to petition the Government for a redress of grievances, and that includes a proposed new tax. The problem is that sometimes meetings start off with a legitimate purpose like that, and then they degenerate into talk about pricing, which is not legitimate. But you say that absolutely didn't happen?" Born asked.

"Absolutely did not. Now we all belong to one or two trade associations, but the trade associations have lawyers that monitor everything that goes on among the competitors. We have a rule that we filter every communication through the trade association lawyers, except when we have a meeting, and in that case the lawyers are present and can step in and shut down any discussion that goes down the wrong path. I seldom, if ever, have had any occasion to send anything to a competitor for trade association committee work or otherwise, but we all know any such communications must go through the lawyer, and he or she can rephrase things, if necessary. I have been told that trade associations can get you in trouble because they are, by definition, a group of competitors. But I don't think we have a problem there," Webb explained.

"Do you ever send out a new price list to your competitors announcing that the attached prices will take place on such-and-such a date, either directly or via the trade association?" Born asked.

"No. We have low-priced products, with thin margins, and it is hard to raise prices, so we cut individual deals with some of our customers, but the last thing we want is for our competitors to find out about our discounts," Webb answered.

"Have you ever had a one-on-one meeting with any Genretta people, like for coffee or lunch, where no one was present except people from Pure Fision and people from Genretta?" asked Born.

"No, I don't think that's ever happened to my best memory. I look on them as enemies, not friends, and that sort of thing just doesn't happen," Webb assured Born.

The interview continued, with Slade affirming that no price-fixing conspiracy ever happened. He said he had never visited socially with any of the Genretta employees and did not even know where they lived. Born scratched his head, "Sounds clean as a whistle to me, but they must think they've got something. Wonder what they think they have. I don't think it is in any of the documents we have produced pursuant to the subpoenas, because we looked at them carefully before producing them and saw nothing."

After finishing his interview with Webb and Evins, being careful not to discuss the results in front of the two Pure Fision officials, Ted and Jamie got in their car and left. They both reported to each other that they turned up nothing that would be incriminating from either of the interviews. "Well, it might just fizzle, maybe the Savannah investigation hasn't gotten as far along as the others, and maybe it will be dropped after all. Or maybe our clients are lying to us. Let's take it one day at a time and see what they've got," Ted said as they continued back to their Greenville office. "Our people will testify before the grand jury next week, and that might tell us something."

Slade Webb and Cranford Evins came out of the grand jury room after being questioned. They were separately debriefed by Ted and Jamie. They each said that no surprise documents were shown to them. However, they were asked the usual questions about whether they had participated in any price-fixing discussions with Genretta employees, to which they both said they absolutely had not. The interesting questions were about whether they had been present when Pure Fision's Savannah manager, Byron Hardy, had engaged in telephone communications with Genretta's Savannah manager. Again, they both

answered "no." Then they were asked if they knew a
man named Drew Acheson. Evins had never heard of
him. Webb said the name sounded familiar but, offhand,
he couldn't place him. Aside from that, the questioning was predictable, and the answers were as Ted and
Jamie expected.

"Seems pretty much like a dud to me," Ted mused
with Jamie. Maybe this one will go away like the others."

CHAPTER FOUR

THE TRUE BILL

The telephone rang in Ted Born's office. He picked up the receiver, with a standard "Hello," but the voice on the other end of the line sounded very matter-of-fact: "Mr. Born, this is Justice Department attorney Jed Fuller, from the Antitrust Division. I wanted to advise you that the grand jury in Savannah yesterday returned a truc bill, an indictment of Pure Fision. You will receive a copy from the office of the Clerk of the Court in due course."

"You sure did take me by surprise with that one! I've been scratching my head trying to figure out why that grand jury had not already been dismissed. I can't find anything through my efforts that would support a conspiracy. Were any individuals indicted along with the company?" Ted asked.

"We obviously think there was collusion, and the grand jury apparently agrees. However, for our own reasons, we did not seek or obtain an indictment against any individuals. We will arrange for a time for the company to enter a plea. Obviously, do not destroy any documents reflecting communications involving the sales department or Genretta, or your company President or Byron Hardy," Fuller advised.

'Which Judge has the case?" Ted asked. The answer was, "Judge Edenton." Ted said he would be in touch with his client about this development and thanked Fuller for the call.

Ted immediately called Jamie Fletcher and asked him to come to his office. "Jamie, we've got bad news. Pure Fision just got indicted by the grand jury in Savannah. We need to call the client immediately." He put in a call to Burton Teague, on his speaker phone, and fortunately was put through to him immediately. "Bad news, Burton. We just got word that your company has been criminally indicted by a Savannah grand jury. I was notified by a JD attorney named Jed Fuller, partly as a courtesy but partly to warn us not to destroy any pertinent documents. I'll give you a list of what I think you need to preserve. If there is any good thing about this indictment, it's that no individuals were hit. That's obviously terribly important, because you sometimes have to make some very hard calls about trying to settle a case when one of your friends or employees might go to jail. Frankly, I think they might have been aiming at Byron, or maybe even you. But no individuals got indicted."

"Why do you think *me*, Ted, and how was I lucky enough to avoid being indicted?" Teague asked.

"Because the Department was very willing to give immunity to your staff, hoping, I'm sure, that they would put the finger on you or Byron, and also, when the JD lawyer called me, he made it a point to say we should not destroy any of your documents, or any of Byron's," Ted responded. "As to why neither of you was personally indicted, I can only surmise that Fuller felt he had enough evidence to implicate the company but not enough to implicate any individuals, and he knew a jury would have more sympathy for a person than for a company. Also, there's a Department of Justice Manual that covers these things. As I recall, it says something like, 'don't indict an individual unless there are at least two witnesses or two strong bits of corroborating evidence.' My guess is, they think they have something on you or Byron, but they didn't feel it was quite enough."

"So, what's next?" Teague asked.

"We pretty well have to resign ourselves that we are going to trial, and pretty fast. You know, under the Sixth Amendment to the Constitution, a defendant is entitled to a 'speedy trial.' This was intended to prevent abuses where a person was held in prison and not given a trial for an extended period of time, frustrating the right to prove one's innocence. To implement this Constitutional requirement, Congress in the 1970s enacted the Speedy Trial Act that requires trials to commence within 70 days of an indictment, with some flexibility where the 'ends of justice' require extensions. But even then, the extensions are very modest. In some situations, the Constitutional requirement has been turned on its head. It works all right when someone was apprehended red-handed robbing a bank, but in a case like ours, it really puts the defendant behind the eight-ball. That's because the Government has unlimited time to bring a charge, even years, and then a defendant is suddenly indicted and has just seventy days to muster a defense.

"In an antitrust case, seventy days is rarely enough, because a lot of documents generally have to be reviewed, and economists have to be hired to express an opinion based on the evidence, and these things take time – to say nothing of the fact that the defense lawyers often are tied up in other pending legal matters and cannot always just drop everything else and focus on getting ready for an important and possibly complicated trial in essentially a few weeks. We have one thing going for us: When we began getting a string of grand jury subpoenas, I hired an economist then, to start looking at the objective data, and he has been at work. When we weren't indicted by the first two or three grand juries, I thought I might have been wasting the company's money. But now I'm really glad we did it, because we have a head-start, and we'll need every bit of it. Of course, we might be able to get a little more time than seventy days, and that would help as well. Still, we are going to have to strive mightily to get ready," Ted explained to a dumbstruck Teague.

"Isn't there something called 'summary judgment,' where you can get rid of a bad case quickly?" Teague asked.

"In civil cases, where there is discovery by both sides, and where many of the facts are not in dispute, yes, you can get rid of a meritless case without having to go to trial, but in criminal cases there essentially is no discovery. The prosecutors do not have to show their hand before trial, and therefore it is usually impossible for you to say the Government has a bad, meritless case, because you never know for sure what evidence the prosecution might have - or claim to have - that you just don't know about. Fat chance of getting rid of the case before going to trial, unless you can show prosecutorial abuse, browbeating of witnesses, improper constituting of the grand jury panel - that kind of thing, which is very hard to prove, because of grand jury secrecy. You usually will not know what went on behind the closed doors to the grand jury room, unless it happens while one of your own witnesses was in the room testifying. We will raise every point we can raise to get your company out of this as soon as we can, but don't count on getting out, especially with the Judge we have," observed Ted.

"What about our Judge? Who is he? Is he bad news?" asked Teague.

"Well, he would not have been my first choice - let's put it that way. Before Judge Edenton was appointed to the Federal bench, there was some sort of scandal – I forget all the details – but he was a lawyer defending white-collar crime cases, and he was accused of some unethical actions. It almost torpedoed his confirmation, but he worked his way out of it and pledged that, if confirmed as a Judge, he would look after the public interest in white-collar crime cases, like ours, and would not be soft on white-collar crime. He has a reputation as a judge of cutting no slack for white-collar defendants. That's not going to make our job any easier," Ted predicted. "We need to plot our strategy immediately, and you can bet we will be keeping you advised. By the way, do you know a fellow named Drew Acheson? His name came up the other day when Slade and Cranford were being questioned before the grand jury."

"No, I don't know him, but I know who he is, and I think Byron used to work with him. Let me see if I can patch Byron in with us," Teague said. "OK, Byron, I've got our lawyer, Ted Born, on the phone. I know you and he have talked about the investigation. He called to tell me our company has been indicted, having to do with our Savannah operations. Isn't that great!! But right now, he has a question about Drew Acheson, and I remember that you've mentioned a few times that you and he used to work together. Will you tell Ted what you know about him? The Government lawyer seemed interested in him."

"Yes, I know him, but I haven't seen him for years and years. Don't see how it could have any bearing on the investigation –," Byron Hardy began.

"Byron, let me interrupt you. It's not an 'investigation' anymore. We've been indicted – the company has – and looks like we're heading for trial, so this is real serious. I am afraid you're going to be spending a lot of time with Ted Born for a while. Now go ahead and finish telling Ted about Drew Acheson," Teague said.

"Damn! What luck! None of the other branches got sued, but mine did. Gosh. All right, back to Drew," Hardy said. "He and I both got our starts working for one of the major soft drink bottlers in Savannah, and we were friends for a couple of years, and then we went our separate ways. I eventually got into the bottled water and energy drink business and, years later, so did he. He was working with Genretta, somewhere down in Florida. I hadn't seen or heard of him for years, and then one day he called me up and said he was in Savannah for a meeting or something, and could we have dinner together, just for old times' sake, to renew our acquaintance. I said 'yes,' but I was wary about it and took some precautions. I brought Slade with me to be a witness in case Drew got out of bounds. But nothing improper happened. All we talked about at the dinner was the old days at the soft drink company – the subject of pricing in the Savannah area never came up – ABSOLUTELY never came up," Hardy recalled.

"Well, that is interesting. But, Byron, do NOT mention this to Slade or any other employees. I don't want the other side cross-examining them and making it appear that you, as their superior, coaxed them to back up your story. We have to be careful how we do things while this case is pending, and it is very important that none of the three of you discuss anything about this case. All right. I've taken up enough of everybody's time for right now, Burton and Byron, but I think we are going to be seeing a lot more of each other in the coming days and weeks. See 'ya," Ted said, as the conversation ended.

He turned to Jamie, who had been taking this all in, though not participating in the phone call, just listening to Ted. "Jamie, we need to see if we can establish when a dinner took place between Byron and Drew Acheson. They used to work together, got together for dinner years after they went separate ways, but Byron says nothing happened. Maybe there are expense reimbursement records, or if we are really lucky, Byron might have written up a little memo about the dinner, for his own protection, or maybe he asked Slade to do it. Or maybe Byron still has his old appointment calendars where we can pinpoint the date. See what you get out of the company's records," Ted instructed.

"If it happened long enough ago, do you think we might have a statute of limitations defense?" Jamie asked.

"Not likely. You see, the law of conspiracy in these criminal cases is very peculiar, at least to my mind. The law generally is that, if a conspiracy is proved to have existed at one point in time, it is presumed to have continued indefinitely until some affirmative action is taken by one or more of the parties to the conspiracy to terminate it. Now, often, if there is a conspiracy, it either never gets off the ground, or else it peters out fairly quickly, because it really is hard to get these conspiracies in place and keep them going. But the law presumes the very opposite. So, if the Government can prove that Byron and Drew made an agreement to fix prices ten years ago, then the law presumes it still continues up to the present – which means at least a part of the conspiracy took place within the period of limitations. And it gets even worse: if any part of the conspiracy is admissible because of occurring within the period of the limitations, then the law lets you go back and prove and rely on the entire so-called conspiracy, not just what took place in the last several years."

The next day, Ted got a copy of the indictment from the Clerk's Office, and he read it over several times and then called Jamie and said, "Before we get too far into the trial preparation for this case, there is something else I think we should do. I've been looking at this indictment, and I've been reading it over and over, and I've been struck by how vague it is. It doesn't state when the alleged conspiracy started or when, or if, it ever ended. It doesn't identify the parties to the so-called conspiracy. It doesn't state where the conspiracy took place or how it came about, nor does it identify any individuals who participated in such conspiracy, or how the conspiracy was carried out. In other words, it just essentially says, 'we charge you with a conspiracy; now come and defend yourself.' I know that prosecutors are allowed lots of lee-way in writing up indictments so as to prevent defendants from manufacturing alibis or false evidence to throw doubt on details of the indictment, especially where the evidence or lack of evidence should be in the hands of the defendant anyway. But, nevertheless, this indictment is so vague I think it should either be thrown out or at least the Court should order the prosecution to serve us with a 'bill of particulars.' It's just not fair to expect us to mount a defense, where criminal liability is at stake, to be followed later with class-action triple damages lawsuits, all on allegations that are ridiculously vague. Even if we don't win, we will hopefully plant in the Judge's mind some sympathy with what we are having to contend with. And the Government needs to understand it has a fight on its hands. This is not going to be one of those quick and easy plea agreements. There's going to be a real fight, based on what I know about the case. Jamie, why don't you try your hand at drafting something for us to go over together. I'll send you the indictment or you can pick it up. Remember, this is a 'due process' issue, whether Pure Fision has gotten due process of law when called upon to defend against these vague allegations."

"We need to be considering other possible pretrial motions as well," Ted continued. "From all I know about this Judge, I doubt he is going to grant any of our motions. He's going to think these motions are just delaying tactics. In his subconscious, he will be thinking the Government wouldn't be bringing the case if Pure Fision wasn't guilty. We have to combat that mindset.

"Assuming we can't dispose of the case via pretrial motions, our best defenses are: NO conspiracy ever happened; and in any case the events the Government relies on took place so long ago, the jury ought to have a reasonable doubt as to the reliability of the memories of those who testify about those long-ago happenings. It is not technically a statute of limitations defense, but it does invoke one of the rationales of every statute of limitations – that after a while, memories just are not sharp enough and reliable enough to be trusted. OK. Let's go to work!" said Ted.

Meanwhile, Ted called the economist he had employed, Dr. Thomas Conrad. "Hi, Tom. I hope you have a little more open time for us, because we are going to need it. Pure Fision has been indicted for price fixing in the Savannah market, and we will be facing an accelerated trial date. I need you to focus especially on the Savannah market, of course. Where do you stand with your research?"

"Good to hear from you, Ted, even if the news is not so good," replied Tom. "I'm gathering all the data I can, but it is not easy to get. I got some from Nielsen, the same company that compiles the TV viewership data. They study the bottled drinks industry in various markets. I have gotten some information also from one of the major soft drink bottlers; they're not selling bottled water or energy drinks at this point, but they have their eye on it and they have been compiling data. Of course, I got some data directly from Pure Fision. I haven't gotten it all put together quite yet, but preliminarily I'm struck by the fact that the prices charged in Savannah are about as low as, if not lower than, they are almost anywhere."

"You will know better than I just where to look," Ted responded, "but let me know if you need our help getting you the cooperation you need from the client in assisting with data or other information. This is serious, and Pure Fision ought to, and does, recognize how serious it is, and I'm confident they will cooperate and be responsive. It sure helps that prices were low in the Savannah area. It would have to be a pretty anemic conspiracy that results in low prices instead of high ones. Still, you can get hammered in the courtroom for anemic conspiracies as well as robust ones. Try to concentrate on the objective data, and then we will get together and go over it all."

CHAPTER FIVE

THE THICKENING PLOT

Ted and Lydia Born were sitting by the window in their breakfast room, Lydia sipping her coffee and Ted savoring his hot tea with lemon. It was a rare oasis of time for them, a Saturday morning when the children had both spent the night with friends, and there was no pressing item on the agenda. Ted smiled, and his eyes met hers, as she returned the smile. The smiles reflected a remembrance and celebration of a beautiful evening they had spent together the evening before, reinforcing their strong mutual feelings of love. They were silent for a moment, communicating only with the glows on their faces. Then Ted looked out the window at the under-construction deck being built in their backyard and reminisced, "Lydia, do you remember the year the house-buying bug bit us and we saw that other house we liked, and the sellers had an asking price of $45,000 for it. We wanted the house but weren't at all sure we could afford it. We finally put in a bid for $42,000, and I could not sleep that night, worried that our bid would be accepted and then we would be committed to something we possibly couldn't afford. We were rescued by someone who met the asking price, and I felt hugely relieved. A little later, we found this house we are living in, which was about $10,000 less expensive, and we bought it. I had been practicing law about four years then - my starting salary was $500 a month in the beginning, tops for this area at the time. You were teaching school and earning even less, but we each contributed $5000 to make a $10,000 down-payment, and we took out a 15-year mortgage for the balance, which is now mostly paid off."

"Yes, I remember all that, with pride," Lydia commented. "Neither of us had ever had much debt, and we were scared to death of it, and still are, I guess. You went to college and law school on academic scholarships, and you worked for your meals. I had inherited a small amount from a great aunt that essentially put me through college. We were stretching to make ends meet a lot of the time, but we had each other. We were in love and committed to each other. We believed in the future, and we made do with old second-hand cars and economized in every way we could. We feel a little more secure now, and I'm glad we made the choices we did, especially the choice to live our lives together."

"You know that I feel exactly the same, maybe even more so. Looking out at this deck we're building, I wonder if we've gotten soft. We really needed a deck to give us some level area in the sloping back yard, but after working with the lumber-marking agencies, and especially with Haywood Norris in the *Balentine* case, I'm sort of obsessed with good quality lumber and using it to build structures the right way. We might be grossly over-building for this house and this neighborhood, but I just couldn't bring myself to take shortcuts with quality. If you want the best lumber for building a deck, you get No. 1 grade Southern yellow pine, and if you want your deck to last forever, you build it by putting the narrow heart-side down and connect them with risers. Of course, that takes a whole lot more lumber, and the labor is a lot more expensive because you have to pre-drill the holes, as it is impossible just to nail through a board from narrow end to narrow end without first pre-drilling a hole for the nails. But, when the carpenters finish this, it's going to be a beauty, and the maintenance should be minimal. Excuse me from wandering from romance to construction, but Jamie Fletcher, who worked with me on the *Ballentine* case and is now working with me on *Pure Fision*, is going to drop by this morning to look at the deck. That case also got him interested in lumber and building, and when he heard what I was doing, he wanted to see it, because virtually nobody builds decks with the narrow edge up, like this one. He might be coming by any minute."

About thirty minutes later, the doorbell rang, and it

was Jamie. "Hi, Jamie, come on in - before we go out," Ted greeted Jamie.

"Hope I didn't come too early," Jamie said. "I'm on my way to the office, want to check something out about our case. I like your house, and I'm sure I'm going to like your deck."

"Come this way, Jamie," Ted directed. "We can walk right through the den and onto the deck. Here it is, not quite finished, but getting there. We still have to put up the railings around the periphery, and we will have benches next to the railing where you can sit if you like. As you can see, it is a two-level deck, with a big hole in the middle to accommodate the giant white oak that comes right up through the hole and provides a good deal of shade for the whole deck. I have this vision of integrating the backyard into a legitimate part of the living area of the house itself – at least a transitional link between indoors and outdoors. I think we're going to have that here."

'Man! Look at these nails going right through the plank from narrow end to narrow end. I've never seen anything like that," exclaimed Jamie. "Fantastic! I am amazed, I really like this. It's like a work of art."

"I have to confess. It is not unique. There are examples here and there, but none in this area that I am aware of. I talked with Haywood Norris about it, and he gave me the idea. You'll have to come back with your bride when it's finished, and we'll have deck furniture and umbrellas, and we can spend some relaxing time together. We will need some relaxation by the time our *Pure Fision* case is over," Ted remarked. "I think Lydia was back in our bedroom when you came in. You can say 'hello' to her in a minute."

"Speaking of the *Pure Fision* case, I picked up something from the rag sheet the soft drink association puts out, that says Genretta's Savannah manager, Paul Sommer, is no longer with Genretta and that his successor has not yet been announced. That's important, because I think it's a sure bet the Government will be calling him as a witness in our case," Jamie shared.

"Wow! That's interesting, Jamie. Thanks for keeping your eyes open. That could be an important bit of information," said Ted.

"I had noticed our law office subscribes to the sheet, maybe compliments of Pure Fision. I don't think many of us pay much attention to it, but I became interested when you got me involved in this case, and I've been scanning it. I'm going to try to find out if the Pure Fision sales staff have picked up any scuttlebutt out in the field about Sommer," Jamie said.

"Exactly, Jamie, please follow up and let me know if you find out anything," Ted counseled. "I'm going to be talking with Genretta's legal counsel also and will see what I can find out that way. Probably not much. I am sure Genretta's got a cooperation agreement with the Government that prevents them from helping us in any way. One other thing. If the Government has any exculpatory evidence, tending to show Pure Fision is not guilty, it is obligated to produce it to us. I don't expect much, but we will see."

Ted and Jamie had worked on their motion to dismiss the indictment of Pure Fision, citing some precedents they thought might persuade the Judge to grant it. The Government filed its opposition, and the Pure Fision team thought it was a bit weak. Nevertheless, the Court denied Pure Fision's motion, without opinion. A few more pretrial motions were filed, all of them summarily slapped down, and the last one was essentially worded as a lecture to Pure Fision and its lawyers to beware of filing any further such motions, saying that, "this case IS going to trial." This Judge is living up to his reputation of being tough on white collar defendants, Ted thought.

After the denial of the initial pretrial motions, Ted Born decided time was passing and he needed to get on the phone with Justice Department attorney Jed Fuller. "Jed, I need a voluntary production of any exculpatory evidence you might have, and I need it quickly so we can avoid having to move for a continuance. Will you agree to produce it voluntarily, or are you going to make me file a motion in Court to get it?" Ted asked.

"I'll have to review all my files to see what, if any-thing I have, and, yes, if I have anything I will produce it voluntarily. You won't have to file anything to get it. Are you contemplating filing for a continuance or are you going to be ready for trial in 70 days?" Fuller countered.

"Jed, I don't mind telling you this indictment was a surprise. I still don't understand it. I'm going to need time with all our witnesses, and we'll have to consider whether we need expert witnesses and how much time the expert would need. I'm not for dragging out this case, but it is really too early for me to say. Of course, I am busy with other matters, and I am sure you are also. I will let you know as soon as I know. By the way, I hear the Genretta manager for Savannah, Paul Sommer, is no longer with Genretta. Do you know anything about that?" Ted asked.

"I'm sorry, but I cannot comment on that. That is an internal matter between the company and Mr. Sommer," Jed answered.

After the call, Ted tried to assess what had just taken place. First, the prosecution was unsure, so they say, as to whether there was exculpatory evidence, which meant to him that there either IS such evidence, or that the prosecution is trying to decide how to classify it. Second, Jed was so guarded about Sommer's departure that it was suggestive of a less than harmonious separation. Ted wondered whether Sommer had been fired and, if fired, the timing might suggest he was let go because of something having to do with this antitrust case and the indictment.

Ted called Jamie. "Jamie, I've just finished talking with Jed at the DOJ. Didn't get much from him except that he's going to check and see if there is any exculpatory evidence, and, if so, he will voluntarily provide it to us. Second, I got the feeling that Sommer's departure from Genretta might not have been a happy one. Since he is no longer an employee of Genretta, we possibly can contact him directly without going through the Genretta attorneys. There's only one catch, and it points out the problems defense counsel have in these criminal cases with the Justice Department. The Department can be quick to claim that any contact with its witnesses is witness tampering. If you probe with the witnesses in a way that suggests you are trying to get them to change their testimony, the Government may claim it is witness tampering, and that not only does not help our client; it also might constitute an alleged crime for which we, as lawyers, are at risk. Now, we haven't been told yet that Sommer is in fact a Government witness, but the circumstances, and especially his former position as head of Genretta operations in Savannah, suggest he could be. This is all so different from civil litigation where defense counsel is obligated to pursue all evidence that might help the client's case. I think I will give Sommer a call and just see what his attitude is. In fact, I think I will do that right now."

There was a white-pages telephone listing for

Sommer, and Ted called the number. Sommer personally answered the call. "Mr. Sommer, I am Ted Born, and I am a lawyer for Pure Fision which has been indicted in the Savannah Federal Court for price fixing. Do you mind if I ask you a few questions?"

"I have been instructed not to speak to anyone about my employment with Genretta or my knowledge of anything relating to Pure Fision, so I will have to hang up the phone and I would request that you not call back or attempt to speak to me or contact me. Thank you," and Sommer hung up the phone on his end. "I think we know now that his instructions came from the Antitrust Division of the Justice Department," and we probably should refrain from further contact. Of course, if he testified before the grand jury, which he probably did, we will get a copy of his testimony before trial. The problem is that you sometimes don't get the testimony until the day the trial begins, and you are tied up in the Courtroom with the trial and do not get a fair chance to read and study it. We need to put a lot of effort into trying to persuade the Judge to order the transmittal of the grand jury transcripts to us no later than the Friday before trial begins on Monday. Even that is late, but it at least gives us a chance to find out something about the Government's case, although it can mean neglecting other trial preparation during the crucial weekend before trial, while we are taking the time to study the grand jury transcripts and determining how to use them."

Ted and Jamie discussed the truncated telephone call with Sommer. "We need to find out everything we can about Sommer – his bio background, who his close friends are, who his neighbors are, and whether he has or is looking for employment. The archives of the social section of the newspaper are a good place to look, because he has been on a bunch of civic boards, and I think he has been head of the United Appeal. Get one of the investigators to check that out," Ted suggested to Jamie.

"Will do," Jamie replied. "But I have already found out something very interesting about that guy Drew Acheson – the one the Government lawyer was asking our people about in the grand jury, and the one our Byron Hardy had dinner with some years back. I was looking at the Antitrust Update publication that we get once a month, new cases and developments in current cases, and I noticed Drew Acheson's name there. Here's the kicker: Acheson has been indicted for price fixing in the Miami area!"

"Hey, do you mean that, you're not kidding?" Ted inquired with his face tense with surprise.

"It's no joke. He's been indicted. I'm guessing he's already made a deal with the Government, like, if you will nol-pros the indictment in Miami, I will sing for you in Savannah," Jamie posited.

"Yeah, you're right on, Jamie, except he might even sing for the Government in Savannah and maybe in other

places, for something less than a full nol-pros dismissal.
Depending on what the Government's got, he might 'cooperate' with them for probation, or even for a lighter
sentence. You know, when the Government's got the
goods on you, and you know you could go to jail and be
thrown in with a bunch of hardcore bad guys, you might
just do anything to get out of it. I know of one case where
an older executive got jail time and they put him in a cell
with some perverts who tried to assault him. That poor
guy ended up committing suicide. What I'm saying is,
the Government has virtually life-and-death control of
you, and the pressure to tell them what they want to hear
can be unbearable. I'm not saying there aren't lawyers
in the DOJ who would not abusively use that pressure
or that there aren't indicted defendants who won't give
in to it, but the potential pressure is hanging over the
whole process, and the defendant's lawyers are probably
advising the executive to cooperate and cut the best deal
possible. The bottom line is, if Acheson is called as a
witness, we have no idea what he might say, but we need
to be prepared for the worst," Ted warned.

CHAPTER SIX

THE EXCULPATORY EVIDENCE

Justice Department attorney Jed Fuller called Ted Born and said, "Ted, I'm responding to your request to furnish you with any exculpatory evidence in our possession, and we have found one document that might be exculpatory, and I am sending it to you by certified mail. As soon as you get it, please acknowledge receipt in writing for my records."

"Certainly," Ted said, "and I appreciate your following through with this. By the way, I think we are going to need some extra time to get ready for this trial. I've got a lot of other cases on my plate, and I need an extra 12 days. Would you be agreeable to that, or at least, would you not oppose it?"

"Not sure, Ted. We might go for 30 days. I'm spending a lot of time here in Savannah, and I need to spend more time in the field office which is the center of everything else I'm working on. Let me think about it, and I'll let you know," Fuller responded. "Of course, the Judge has a mind of his own and seems to tightly control his docket, so he might or might not be in a mood to make any changes, whatever you and I agree to."

"I understand it's all up to the Judge, Jed. But this is not your everyday criminal case. It involves economics and other things. I know that, in the end, we obviously do whatever the Judge says. But I think it would help if we could agree on it. Just think about it and we can talk some more at a later time – but not too much later. I have a feeling Judge Edenton might not appreciate last minute motions for continuances."

In a few days, Ted opened his mail and found the document Jed Fuller had promised. It was a short one-paragraph affidavit, signed under oath by Acheson stating that he had no knowledge or information as to any price fixing in the Savannah area. "This is great stuff!" Ted was telling himself. It would seem to take Acheson out of the picture as a potential witness for the Government, and it confirmed what Pure Fision's own employees were telling Ted and Jamie. "Let's see, now. Acheson was the head guy over the Miami and Savannah operations of Genretta, plus some other areas of Florida and Georgia. Byron Hardy was the head of Pure Fision's

70

Savannah operations. They both swear there was no conspiracy. Our other Fision employees say they know of no conspiracy. The prices in the marketplace don't suggest any conspiracy. That means the Government's whole case rests on Paul Sommer. He must have admitted to a conspiracy of some sort, probably caused him to be fired. I'm assuming there's no documentary evidence of price fixing. At least I haven't seen any. But if Sommer is the whole basis of the indictment, and if it's his word against ours, the Government's case is incredibly flimsy. In fact, I think it would be against Justice Department policy to indict in such a situation. It just doesn't add up. In any case, it looks like we need to focus on Sommer. I will call Jamie and see if we can expedite the investigation of Sommer."

A preliminary investigative report was in Ted's hands within a few days. It reported that Sommer was about 45 years old, was born in the Midwest, had graduated from the University of Wisconsin where he played football. After college, he was in the military for a couple of years, then had a series of sales jobs, married, and eventually had three children. He went to work for Genretta in Maryland as a salesman, then came up through the ranks to be a manager of some smaller Genretta operations. Finally, Genretta sent him to Savannah to run its shop down there. He and his family took to Savannah, apparently loved the place and jumped right into civic and community organizations. He seems to have been a competent manager, but he earned a reputation with his employees as being quick-tempered and ran the business somewhat like a drill sergeant. His relationship with his local employees was distant and demanding. He was not at all gregarious or buddy-buddy with employees, kept his own counsel for the most part. He had a sales manager, Eric Smith, who seemed to have had more contact with him than other employees. He seems not to have had close friendships with his neighbors, and none of them seemed to have any knowledge of why he was no longer with Genretta. However, it seems he was still unemployed and appeared to hang around his house most of the time.

Ted called Byron Hardy, went over the investigative report with him, and probed Hardy's relationship with Sommer. Hardy said, "I first ran into Sommer in a grocery store. I had stopped in the grocery store on my way to the office to check on whether we were getting the shelf space that had been promised us. Sommer was there checking on his own displays. We introduced ourselves, said 'Hello,' 'How are you?' and I think I said, 'I hope you've enjoyed Savannah,' or something like that. It lasted for less than a couple of minutes, and I was back in my car, heading to the office. After that, we had a few occasions to talk. One time, one of our salespersons literally got into a fight with a Genretta salesman, and we both had to calm down the situation and deal with our employees, and we spoke on the phone about it. Then, there was a proposed tax on soft drink products. I was obviously opposed to the tax in the first place, but if the Legislature was going to pass some type of tax, a fallback

position for us was that the tax should be strictly limited to soft drinks, not including bottled water or energy
drinks. We talked about how we had common ground on
the tax issues and needed to contact representatives in the
legislative chambers with our opposition.

"I had only one occasion where we were ever together. We accidentally ran into each other, and I needed a
ride home. He offered me a ride and suggested we have
a drink during happy hour at the Tiger's Den. We talked
about Savannah, and Sommer said he would like to join
the Yacht Club but knew it had a long waiting list. He
said he sometimes would take a break from his office and
just go down to the river walk and feel the great breeze
that generally came in off the ocean. That's all that
happened, lasted a total of maybe thirty minutes, and
then he took me on home. I assure you there was no talk
of price fixing."

"Well, I believe you, but I have to assume Sommer
is going to tell a different story. Think back about the
Tiger's Den incident, and let's get into that in more detail.
Otherwise, I cannot imagine a basis for a criminal prosecution," Ted mused. "I guess we'll find out."

"I do have a confession to make, though, Ted," Byron
said ominously. "You had told us from the beginning that
Slade and Cranford and I should not talk together about
this case or about any knowledge we had about price fixing. We stuck to your advice to a 'T' in the beginning of

the grand jury hearings, but then they called Slade back to the grand jury a second time, and in doing so, they strongly implied that he had not told the truth at his first hearing, and he knew he had immunity only if he told the truth. So, he sweated it and seemed almost to have a nervous breakdown over it, and he got Cranford and me together and said, 'I have been wracking my brain to see if I can remember anything that has happened that could be price fixing, and I can't think of a thing. But the Government thinks I'm lying, and I'm afraid they know something that I've forgotten, and I don't want to go to jail. Is there anything either of you know that I might have forgotten?' Slade was almost a basket case. I told him the only thing I knew was the Tiger's Den happy hour drinks together. I have the impression that Slade mentioned this to the grand jury in his second appearance. He says he never testified this was price fixing, but he was so nervous I'm not sure how it came out," Byron confessed.

"Byron, I didn't even know he had been called back to the grand jury. This is all news to me, and not good news. Why did you not call me?" Ted asked.

"Actually, I did try to call you. But you were out of town, and we knew you couldn't be with Slade in the grand jury room anyway, and the Government lawyers told him they had just a few questions, so Slade wanted to go on by himself and get it over with. I know it shouldn't have happened that way, but I guess now we need to confess and tell you about it."

"We'll need to talk with Slade and get more information on what he said in his second grand jury session,"
Ted says. "Remember, Byron, we are on your side. Please
don't keep any secrets from us. If there are any other
things that have happened that we don't know about,
please, please let us know NOW. The worst thing that
can happen is to be taken by surprise in the Courtroom
in the middle of trial. We can't afford to be ambushed.
I will call Slade and we will get together as soon as possible, hopefully tomorrow, and in the meantime do NOT
talk to Slade or Cranford or anyone in your organization
about anything bearing on price fixing or this criminal
case. And call me if you get tempted."

Slade was available the next day, and Ted met with
him. "Slade, we have to know, according to your honest
best recollection, what you were asked and what you said
to the grand jury when you were called the second time.
Now, remember, there was a court reporter in that grand
jury room taking down everything you said, and they can
bring that transcript out in Judge Edenton's Courtroom
and make you read the testimony you gave the grand jury.
So don't let me be surprised. Whatever you said, good or
bad, I need to know."

"I'm sorry, Ted," Slade apologized. "I know I did
wrong, but you can't imagine how scared and worried I
was. They asked me again if I knew of any meetings or
conversations between anyone at Pure Fision and anyone
connected with Genretta, and had I been able to refresh

my memory. I told them I had told the truth as best I could remember, but I now knew of a meeting that took place, and I told them about the Tiger's Den meeting."

"What did you tell them about that meeting?" Ted asked.

"I didn't know what to say. I just said I heard there had been this meeting, that I wasn't even at the meeting. Of course, I was very nervous, and I can't say for sure exactly how it all came out. I hope I didn't do any harm," Slade replied with contrition.

"I understand how it was, Slade. Just try to relax. As far as I can tell, the Government's case is not a strong one, but what bothers me is what we don't know. Does the Justice Department have information we don't have? That's the danger. What's done is done. We'll just have to deal with it, and we will. Get yourself calm, and know we are going to do everything possible to protect you and the company."

Ted went back to the office and met with Jamie Fletcher. Jamie had just come out of a meeting with a new client of Ted's, Anson Fowlkes, President and owner of a company named AFCO. Ted had already met briefly with Fowlkes, but he had asked Jamie to do an in-depth debriefing of him concerning all the facts, while Ted was focused on the *Pure Fision* case. Ted brought Jamie up to date on developments in the latter case, including the exculpatory affidavit and the surprise second grand jury appearance of Slade Webb. "I think I will call the Genretta lawyer to see if he has any insight into the exculpatory affidavit. Since the affidavit says there was no collusion, Genretta should not have any problem verifying that fact - and possibly even arranging for an interview with Acheson."

Ted called Genretta's lawyer and attempted to discuss the Acheson affidavit. The lawyer stated his client had a cooperation agreement with the Government, and he could not discuss the affidavit. Ted probed as to why not, since the affidavit did not advance the Government's case. The lawyer said, "Look, we hope you win the case, because if you lose, both companies are going to be sued in a class action for treble damages and attorneys' fees – could be millions of dollars. But we have an agreement to cooperate with the Government, and all kinds of things would be jeopardized if we are considered to have breached that agreement."

"But the affidavit says there was no collusion, no conspiracy, no price fixing. How could you go wrong just discussing something like that?" Ted asked.

"Well," the lawyer responded, "he did say all those things, but then later he said something else. That's all I can tell you."

"You are saying he recanted, that he took back what he had said in his affidavit!" Ted exclaimed.

"You need to draw your own conclusions. Now I have

to hang up. Goodbye," he said.

Ted struck his palm to his forehead. "It was all a trap! A setup! These DOJ lawyers sent me this so-called exculpatory affidavit by Acheson, hoping we would get ourselves out on a limb and then they would cut us down, embarrass us before the jury, and say Acheson was lying in the first affidavit, but his revised affidavit was true! What dirty tactics! This was an act intended to mislead and entrap us, by not telling us the whole story. I can't ever trust them again."

Jamie was listening, and said, "Maybe the Government has more to support its case than we thought. That's why we had a hard time figuring out how the Government could bring a case based on what we thought was skimpy evidence. Now we know they've got more. How much more, we still don't know."

The Judge reluctantly gave the parties three more weeks to get ready for trial, with the admonition that no further extensions would be granted for any reason, looking sternly at Ted Born. Born and Fletcher worked feverishly with their witnesses, going over the expected testimony. One of the decisions that had to be made was what individual would serve as the "company representative" to sit at the counsel table during trial, the purpose being to give the defense lawyers access to a real live person familiar with the defendant's business, for quick consultation relative to issues that might arise.

Normally, it would be someone at or near the top, like Burton Teague or Byron Hardy, head of the Savannah operations. However, Ted knew that jurors would be looking at the company rep through the entire trial and would get their subconscious feelings about the company from the corporate rep, and Ted feared that Hardy was a bit stiff and distant, not an ideal company rep. The logical alternative was Slade Webb, who was a salt-of-the-earth-common-touch sort of guy, and he was the head of sales, a critical issue in the trial. The problem with Slade was that he was the one who had broken down under pressure from the prosecution at the grand jury stage and had become so nervous he caused the three key defense witnesses to break Ted's instructions not to discuss the case among themselves. However, the more Ted and Jamie worked with Slade, the better they felt about his ability to handle himself, and so Slade was the choice – much to Byron Hardy's relief.

One of the pieces of evidence the defense needed was the separation agreement between Genretta and Paul Sommer. Ted felt there surely would be such a document, and that the document would, among other things, cover the reasons for the separation - probably firing - of Sommer. Whatever it said, Ted felt he could probably use it to Pure Fision's advantage, and in any case, it was something the defense needed to know. There being no discovery in a criminal case, Ted could not get the document *before* trial, but he could subpoena Genretta to produce the document *at* trial, so the subpoena was prepared and served on Genretta. The defense also obtained copies of the indictment of Drew Acheson in Miami.

The Judge had ordered the Government lawyers to turn over the grand jury transcripts of all witnesses the Government intended to call, but only at the end of the day on Friday before the trial would begin on the following Monday. The transcripts included testimony of Paul Sommer, Drew Acheson and Genretta sales manager Eric Smith; it did not include the testimony of Pure Fision employees who testified, so the defense would have to rely on the accuracy of the debriefing of Slade Webb and Cranford Evins. It was a frantic weekend, trying to analyze the three transcripts and do everything else that needed to be done. All exhibits had to be pre-marked. Ted was working with a jury selection analyst to prepare for striking the jury, who urged him to strike potential jurors who were talkative (they would dominate the jury deliberations) as well as those who seemed submissive to authority and might feel that, if the Government accused you of price fixing, you are guilty because otherwise you wouldn't be indicted. The jury consultant also warned against people who had been convicted of crimes or had family members who had been convicted, but she also noted that the Government would strike such persons anyway, so don't waste a strike on them. "You want intelligent jurors, who will think for themselves and won't readily swallow everything the Government witnesses say," she advised.

Ted had also decided to let Jamie make the opening statement, which the two of them had rehearsed many times. Everything had to come together just right for a proper defense.

The good thing was that there was a lot of helpful information in the grand jury transcripts.

CHAPTER SEVEN

THE TRIAL BEGINS

The Judge did not allow a jury questionnaire, nor were counsel allowed to conduct a *voir dire* questioning of the jury venire. The Judge asked the usual questions and then allowed counsel to suggest to him additional questions that might be asked of the prospective jurors to enable counsel to decide which of them to strike. One good thing for a defendant is that the defense side in a criminal trial, unlike a civil trial, is given two strikes for every strike by the prosecutors. A lot of this process, under the given format, resulted in relatively blind striking, not having enough information to make strikes with confidence, mainly trying to read body language, looking for relatively positive facial expressions rather than sour or bored expressions. All things considered, the jury looked all right, at least not scary. There were six men and six women, five African Americans and seven Caucasians, plus two alternates who would hear the trial but would be excused from service before deliberations began, unless one or more of the regular jurors was unable to finish out the trial.

The Judge explained to the jury that the Government lawyer, Mr. Fuller, would give his opening statement first, because the Government had the burden of proof, and called upon Jed Fuller to proceed.

"Ladies and Gentlemen, I am Jed Fuller, a lawyer with the United States Justice Department. This trial is taking place because a grand jury has heard testimony and reviewed evidence and, on that basis, has returned an indictment against Pure Fision for committing the offense of price fixing in the bottled water and energy drink market in the Savannah area. That means Pure Fision is accused of colluding with one or more or its competitors to set the prices of its products to eliminate or reduce competition, and thereby to take advantage of consumers through artificial pricing, rather than prices determined by fair and honest competition. We, as lawyers for the Government, are here to present evidence to you that such price fixing in fact did occur.

We have witnesses, whose testimony you will hear, who observed such price fixing and may have participated in it. It is not a complicated case. All you have to do is to decide if one or more price-fixing agreements occurred, and if so, that would establish guilt even if the parties to the price fixing never followed through on it. The witnesses you will hear from are credible and there is no reason to believe that they are not telling the truth. Consumers have the right to feel secure that, when they buy bottled water or energy drinks, or anything else, that they can expect to get charged a price set by marketplace competition and not by collusion. We are prosecuting this case to ensure that fair and non-collusive pricing prevails when you buy bottled water or energy drinks." Looking at his notes, Fuller said, "That's really all I need to say at this time, even though I have not used all the time allotted to me. I think what we need to do is to let you hear from the witnesses themselves, and then I will address you in a closing argument at the end of the trial, after you have heard what we believe will be compelling evidence. Thank you." Jed Fuller took his seat.

The Judge then said, "And now the attorneys for the defendant, Pure Fision, will make an opening statement." Ted Born rose and said, "Your Honor, my associate James Fletcher will present the opening statement on behalf of Pure Fision."

Jamie Fletcher rose, looking the jurors in the eye and using no notes. "May it please the Court. Ladies and gentlemen, I am honored to be here and make this opening statement to you, which I hope will be helpful. We appreciate very much your service in this trial. At this point, you have heard no evidence at all. You have heard some accusations from Mr. Fuller, but his accusations are not evidence. If I were to ask you right now whether you think Pure Fision is guilty of price fixing, every one of you should say our client is innocent, 'not guilty,' because in our system of justice defendants are presumed innocent, until by the evidence they are found guilty *beyond a reasonable doubt*. The Court will give you instructions about this at the close of trial. But you start this trial with a 100% presumption that Pure Fision is innocent, and that presumption can only be changed if you find the evidence strong enough so that you don't have any reasonable doubt that it is guilty. Furthermore, it is the Government that has the burden of proving guilt. We really don't have to prove anything. The Government has the laboring oar to prove guilt beyond a reasonable doubt.

"Now, I want to be sure you understand, while we are pointing out the presumption of innocence and the prosecution's burden of proof beyond a reasonable doubt, that this is not the main thrust of our defense of Pure Fision. Our strong and emphatic position is that no price-fixing occurred. The Government has big problems with its case. In the first place, there are very, very serious credibility problems with their witnesses. Did you hear Mr. Fuller tell you the Government had no reason not to tell the truth? We submit to you that they had powerful reasons *not* to tell the truth, including the fact that the Government has made a deal with them to provide testimony in exchange for not being prosecuted and possibly put in jail. Our witnesses are the ones who will tell you in no uncertain terms that no price fixing took place. In addition, the idea there was collusion is not going to make any sense to you when you have heard the evidence, because we are going to prove to you that the retail prices paid by consumers for bottled water and energy drinks were the lowest and cheapest in the Savannah area of any region in the Southeast, and possibly in the entire country. Now, why in the world would Pure Fision collude with someone to fix prices and then sell at the cheapest prices available anywhere? People don't collude in order to charge rock bottom prices; if you collude, it is for the purpose of raising prices, charging high prices. So, you are called on here in this Courtroom to use your common sense and judgment in evaluating whether you believe what each witness is saying, and you should ask yourselves, 'Does it make sense?' Can you believe beyond a reasonable doubt that collusion occurred when the prosecution's witnesses have every reason to say what the prosecutors want them to say, and when the results are totally inconsistent with their testimony?

"There is also a further issue in this case, called the statute of limitations. We have laws that prevent cases like this one from being filed if the events took place a very long time ago. The statute of limitations in this case is five years – a very generous statute of limitations, as most statutes of limitations are much shorter than that. This just means that the acts of which the defendant is accused must have taken place within the last five year before the indictment. There is a very good reason why we have statutes of limitation, because after the passage of years, memories are not as reliable as in more recent times, and often the evidence a defendant needs for defense has disappeared and is no longer available. So there has to be a cutoff, and that cutoff in this type of case is five years. Much of the evidence you will hear in this case, in fact almost all of it, took place longer than five years ago, some of it as long ago as ten years. The Government is going to try to convince you that the so-called collusion started as long ago as ten year and continued up to a time less than five years ago. We expect the evidence to show that, even if there had ever been a conspiracy – which Pure Fision strongly denies - it stopped and ended, by the testimony of the Government's own witnesses, more than five years before any indictment in this case. So please take note of the time periods when the Government claims there was a conspiracy, because we are confident there will not be any relevant evidence of a continuous conspiracy that extended into the most recent five-year period. I think that is about as far as I need to go right now. But as you hear and consider the testimony, remember the presumption of innocence, the burden of proof beyond a reasonable doubt, the credibility of the witnesses, and the time frames involved. After the Government concludes its case, Pure Fision will have an opportunity to present its own witnesses, and we ask you to weight all the testimony on a presumption of innocence/beyond-a-reasonable-doubt standard, and we believe you will conclude that Pure Fision is not guilty in this case. Thank you for the close attention that I see you are giving to this case."

The Judge then addressed the Courtroom: "Ladies and gentlemen of the jury, you have just heard the opening statements of the Government prosecution and the Pure Fision defense. Please bear in mind that nothing you have so far heard from either side is evidence in this case, and remember that the law you are to use in making your findings at the end of trial will come from me as the Judge in this case and may or may not be exactly what either of the lawyers has told you. But you must base your decision on the evidence allowed in this Courtroom and on the law that I will instruct you about. As you have been told, the prosecution, which has the burden of proof, puts on its evidence first, and I ask Mr. Jed Fuller to call his first witness for the prosecution."

Fuller called Paul Sommer, the former division manager for Genretta. After establishing that Genretta sold bottled water and energy drinks in various parts of the United States and that Genretta was a competitor of Pure Fision, Fuller asked Sommer if he had ever been a party to any price-fixing agreement with Pure Fision. Sommer - with head mainly looking downward – said that, yes, he had once met Byron Hardy, Savannah manager of Pure Fision, in the Tiger's Den lounge or bar, where they had met for the purpose of exchanging retail price lists that each had prepared for circulating to their customers in the next day or two. He had previously talked with Hardy on the phone, he said, and they had decided prices were too low and needed to be raised and they decided to rendezvous at the Tiger's Den. Sommer could not remember who suggested the situs for the meeting. According to Sommer, they each had a drink, and then they went their separate ways. He testified he thought the meeting had occurred in the spring of 1983. He said just after that meeting that he got directives from his home office, in no uncertain terms, that there should be no more collusion, and that it stopped at that point. He said he had from time to time talked via telephone with Pure Fision's representatives, including one occasion when he went to the apartment occupied by Pure Fision's Savannah sales manager, Slade Webb, to hand him a retail price list Genretta was about to circulate to customers. He was clear that no collusion took place after the spring of 1983, and identified only vague telephone calls before that time, plus the alleged meeting with Hardy in the Tiger's Den in the spring of 1983. He testified that he was no longer employed by Genretta, but was not asked any questions beyond that, about the circumstances of his leaving, or whether he was now employed elsewhere. Fuller tendered the witness for cross-examination.

Ted Born rose. "Mr. Sommer, I don't believe we have ever met, but I am Ted Born, a lawyer for Pure Fision. I did, however, telephone you, did I not, to see if you would discuss with me what you knew about this case. Do you remember that?"

Sommer: "Yes."

Born: "And you hung up the phone on me, refusing to speak to me, did you not?"

Sommer: "Yes. Mr. Fuller told me not to talk with any Pure Fision representative."

Born: "But you did speak to Mr. Fuller, the Government lawyer, and you gave testimony before the grand jury, did you not?"

Sommer acknowledged that he had. "Were you given immunity from prosecution for your testimony, protecting you from being a defendant like Pure Fision is?"

"Yes, except that I got immunity only if I told the truth," Sommer replied.

Born: "You've testified you had a meeting with Mr. Byron Hardy, and you stated that it was a pre-arranged meeting where you each brought a set of price lists with you and exchanged them. Are you quite sure about that, Mr. Sommer?"

Sommer: "The best I can remember."

Born: "Do you remember that in fact you and Mr. Hardy ran into each other by accident at a political rally, that Mr. Hardy had locked his keys in his car, and you offered to drive him home after the rally so he could get another set of keys and unlock his car?"

Sommer: "I remember that happened, not sure whether it was the same occasion or not." Sommer was looking down.

Born: "And you suggested that the two of you stop by the Tiger's Den and have a drink?"

"We decided to stop and have a drink, not sure who suggested it," Sommer said.

Born: "Then it was not a prearranged meeting at all, was it? And there was no exchange of price lists was there?"

Sommer: "I'm having trouble remembering. There wouldn't have been any price exchanges at that meeting, but I am not sure whether there was another Tiger's Den meeting."

Born: "Now, please think back, Mr. Sommer. There was only one Tiger's Den occasion, wasn't there?"

Sommer: "It seems like maybe there was just one, but now that I think about it, I'm not sure."

Born: "You say there was collusion. Did a time come when any such collusion ended?"

Sommer: "Yes. I got strict instructions from the Genretta top management, right after the Tigers Den meeting, that there should be no more price fixing, and so we stopped. And that would have been late 1982 or the spring of 1983."

Born: "And are you saying that there was a complete termination of any collusion at that point, and if any occurred later, that would have been a new beginning?"

Sommer: "Right. The collusion ended, and if anything started up, it would have been a new deal."

Born: "And that's what you told the grand jury as well, isn't it?" Sommer acknowledged that he thought it was. Born continued, "I would like you to think back with me, Mr. Sommer. You remember that you and Mr. Hardy encountered each other, without any prearrangement, at a political rally prior to an election, and that led to the Tiger Den meeting after the rally. Am I right about that?"

Sommer: "That's right, as I remember it now."

Born: "Who was the politician who was holding the rally?"

Sommer: "I think that it was our Congressman, running for re-election to Congress."

Born: "So that would have been a Federal election, and Federal elections always take place in even-numbered years, do they not?"

Sommer: "That's right."

Born. "So, the rally would have been sometime before November 1982, not 1983, right?"

Sommer: "I guess I would have to agree, yes, it would have had to have been before the November election of that year."

Born: "And that means all collusion, if there had ever been any, had come to a complete stop and had completely ended before November 1982."

Sommer: "Or thereabouts. I would say before the end of 1982."

Born: "You were asked by the Government lawyer about several announcements of new price lists that occurred from time to time, were you not?"

Sommer: "Yes."

Born: "Do your customers pay you the prices on your price lists?"

Sommer smiled. "Almost nobody pays the 'official' price list. We discount to customers off that list, and the discounts run the gamut among our customers – whatever we can get, depending on the competition."

Born: "And you mainly competed against Pure Fision based on the discounted price, not the list price, right?"

Sommer: "Yeah, that's the way it actually works."

Born: "And the competition at the discounted price was fierce, wasn't it?"

Sommer: "No question about it. It was fierce,

all the time."

Born: "I gather then, that there was essentially no collusion at the level where the customer actually was charged, because that was always fiercely competitive?"

Sommer: "Well, there might have been mention made, at times, that there was too much discounting going on, but the discounted prices were all over the lot, and there were too many of them to police, so in essence we just competed, sometimes blindly, because we couldn't usually verify the price our customers claimed they were paying Pure Fision, and we just did the best we could to get the business."

Born: "You had a sales manager who worked under you who had responsibility for pricing your products to customers, subject to your oversight, of course. Did you ever bring him into any discussions about fixing prices with Pure Fision?"

Sommer: "Honestly, no. He dealt mainly with approving discounts, and there was never any practical way to coordinate that with the competition, so I never brought him in. I mainly was dealing with Pure Fision on price lists, a few times."

Born: "You said in answer to Mr. Fuller's questions that you once took a proposed price list to the apartment of Slade Webb, the sales manager of Pure Fision in the Savannah area. Did you know Mr. Webb personally at that time?"

Sommer: "I didn't really know him. I think I had seen him somewhere before."

Born: "Do you remember when that was, or can you relate it to any event that would help date it?"

Sommer: "I can't remember at this point. Seems like the weather was kind of cool, could have been late fall or winter, but that is the best I can do."

Born: "Did you actually see Mr. Webb when you went to his apartment?"

Sommer: "I don't think so. I think I either gave it to his wife or I slipped it under his door."

Born: "Did Mr. Webb ask you to bring the price list?"

Sommer: "I don't recall. But I thought it would help in the market if he knew what we were planning. There had been other times when price lists were exchanged between the companies, and this was just a specific instance I can remember."

Born: "Do you remember where the apartment was?"

Sommer: "Not exactly. Somewhere not far from the Pure Fision office, as I recall."

Born: "Did you actually implement or publish the price list to customers after that?"

Sommer: "Probably did. Don't ask me whether Pure Fision followed up with a release of a comparable price list increase. It's been a long time, and I don't remember."

Born: "Wouldn't it have been easier just to pick up the telephone and tell Mr. Webb what you were planning to do with the price increases? Why did you have to make a trip to Mr. Webb's apartment?"

Sommer: "I just didn't know Mr. Webb that well at the time. I think he was new on the job. I guess I just felt this was a more personal way to make contact with him."

Born: "Did you involve Mr. Webb in any price list exchanges after that occasion?"

Sommer: "No. I think my other contacts were with his boss, Byron Hardy."

Born: "But you never brought your own sales manager in on any of the price list exchanges or even told him they were occurring?"

Sommer: "No, I wanted to keep it all tight, just me at the top."

Born: "And yet you say you took the price list to Slade Webb on this occasion. Why not to the top of Pure Fision's Savannah operations, Byron Hardy?"

Sommer: "I think I had heard that Mr. Hardy was out of town. That's the best I can remember. I did have other contacts with Mr. Hardy at other times."

Born: "Let's take those other contacts, one-by-one and tell us about each one of them."

Sommer: "I can't do that. It's been so long ago. Some were on the telephone. That was mostly the way. I mainly was looking to get a reaction from Mr. Hardy as to whether he was positive or negative about a price increase. Sometimes it wasn't necessary to actually tell him exactly what we planned to do. I just needed to get a feel for where I thought he would probably stand in terms of a need for a price increase. Sometimes I would call him about trade association business, and I would slip in a comment about a need for price increases, just to get a feel for his reaction."

Born: "Did Mr. Hardy - or anyone connected with Pure Fision - ever initiate telephone calls or other contacts to talk with you or mention price increases?"

Sommer: "He might have, but I can't really remember any specific occasion. You see, they got into the market first and had the lion's share when I arrived in Savannah. So, I was always trying to take market share away from Pure Fision. At the same time, I would need to increase my prices because I was always selling just a hair above my costs. If I went up on my prices and Pure Fision didn't, I would lose market share. So, to get needed price increases without sacrificing market share, I needed to know whether Pure Fision would follow us. So, most of the time, I guess I would initiate the contacts with Mr.

Hardy. It was awkward because I did not know him well, and I was having to dance around the subject, but still try to make progress until I got orders from the home office that it had to stop."

Born: "Mr. Sommer, have you told us everything you know or can remember about any contacts or communications between Genretta and Pure Fision about product pricing."

Sommer: "To the best of my memory. We're talking about things that happened five-to-ten years ago."

At that point the Court decided to break the proceedings for the day and resume the next morning.

When proceedings got underway the following morning, Born was beginning to resume his questioning when Sommer said, "I would like to clarify something I said yesterday. When I got the orders from the home office to cease all price contacts with Pure Fision, I think there were some contacts that still went on, but on a reduced basis. I just wanted to say that."

Ted Born paused for a moment, looked at the jury, saw some frowns, and then he asked: "Mr. Sommer, did you have an opportunity to talk with the Government lawyers yesterday after we broke for the day?"

Sommer looked at the Government's table, paused, looked down, and said, "I don't remember."

Born: "Mr. Sommer, you have been talking about things you could more or less remember from five-to-ten years ago, but you can't remember whether you talked with the Government's lawyers at the conclusion of your testimony yesterday?"

Sommer: "This whole thing has made me very nervous. So much has happened. I just can't remember."

Born: "One or more of the Government lawyers told you to come in today and make that statement as a 'correction' to your testimony of yesterday, isn't that true?"

Sommer: "I just can't remember, like I said."

Born: "Are you saying your testimony yesterday was untruthful, when you testified all communications on pricing had ceased as of the end of 1982, and if anything happened after that time, it was a 'new beginning'?"

Sommer: "I'm just doing the best I can. I can't get every detail just right all the time."

Born: "Are there other things you said yesterday that were incorrect, that you need to correct?"

Sommer: "Not that I can think of."

Born: "Mr. Sommer, let me try to refresh your recollection. Didn't one of the Government lawyers tell you that the Government would have statute of limitations problems with this case if you did not change your testimony?"

Sommer, looking down: "I can't remember."

Ted Born looked at the jury and then quickly completed his cross-examination. Fuller, for the prosecution,
followed by just a couple of questions seeking to confirm
that some pricing coordination had occurred between
Genretta and Pure Fision, even if he could not remember all the details. Sommer obligingly said that it had.
The questioning of Mr. Sommer was then concluded, but
Ted Born asked the Court to order Mr. Sommer to be
available for further questioning during the defense's part
of the case, as he could be needed to authenticate documents as a part of the defense's case, the Court having
ruled that no defense documents could be admitted in
evidence during the prosecution's presentation of its part
of the case.

The Government lawyers next called Mr. Eric Smith
as the next witness. Anita Scribe, an associate of Jed
Fuller, conducted the questioning of Mr. Smith. Mr.
Smith acknowledged that he had no direct knowledge or
involvement in any price-fixing conspiracy. However,
he did say that he had been present in the office of his
boss, Mr. Sommer, when Sommer had been talking with
someone that he assumed was Byron Hardy. He assumed
it was Hardy with whom Sommer was talking, because
Sommer had asked him - Smith - to close the office door,
interpreted by Smith as a sign that a highly sensitive and
confidential discussion was taking place. Smith could
only hear Sommer's part of the telephone conversation,

and indeed only a portion of that, as he had left the room before the conversation was concluded. He said Sommer had told him afterward that "everything was all right." Jamie Fletcher objected to this testimony as hearsay and irrelevant, and he moved to strike it, because Smith never had direct knowledge of the identity of the person to whom Sommer was speaking or the gist of the conversation. The Judge, at a side bar conference dealing with the motion to strike, questioned the value of the testimony but noted that otherwise hearsay testimony was admissible if it came from one party to a conspiracy, assuming a conspiracy was proven. On the possibility that other evidence might later show the relevance of this testimony, the Judge allowed it to stand, at least for the time being.

Ted and Jamie could not see why the Government called Smith as a witness, as he verified that he, as sales manager knew of no conspiracy and had not participated in one, and, further, that his overhearing bits of one end of a conversation without actual knowledge of who was on the other end was so weak that it seemed to be more of a negative for the Government's case than a positive. Apparently, the prosecution thought it provided some circumstantial evidence of collusive contacts, making Sommer's testimony more credible.

The Government's third witness was Drew Acheson, the former regional manager for Genretta, whose area of responsibility had been the Florida and Georgia areas for a couple of years, including Savannah. He related that he and Byron Hardy had had a dinner conversation at a hotel restaurant about ten years earlier which culminated in an agreement for the two companies, Genretta and Pure Fision, to coordinate and raise pricing. Shortly afterward, according to Acheson, he had changed jobs and had gone back to work with a soft drink company, and he had no information as to what had happened in the Savannah market thereafter.

Ted Born rose to cross-examine Acheson. "Mr. Acheson, you had known Mr. Hardy for many years, going back to a time you both worked together for a soft drink company, and you considered him a personal friend. Is that correct?"

Acheson: "Yes, that is correct. I thought a lot of Byron Hardy."

Born: "And you telephoned Mr. Hardy and asked him to have dinner with you, because you were in Savannah briefly and you wanted to renew your long friendship, or at least that's what you told Mr. Hardy, is it not?"

Acheson: "Yes, I told him that, and I was sincere, although I hoped perhaps it might also serve Genretta's interests, if things went well."

Born: "Let's see if I understand this: You initiated the telephone call, not Mr. Hardy. You extended the invitation to dinner, not Mr. Hardy's idea or doings. You did all of this under a guise of friendship, with no mention to Mr.

Hardy that the subject of price fixing might come up?"

Acheson: "That's essentially correct, I would say."

Born: "That event took place a long time ago, like ten years ago, didn't it?

Acheson: "Something like that, not sure exactly."

Born: "Do you remember where you had dinner?"

Acheson: "I'm sorry. I'm not sure about that."

Born: "Did you have alcoholic beverages to drink and, if so, how many?"

Acheson: "Normally, I would have a couple of glasses of white wine with dinner, so I assume that's what I had. I can't remember the details of what Byron might have drunk."

Born: "Was there anyone else having dinner at the same table with the two of you?"

Acheson: "No, just the two of us."

Born: "Are you quite sure of that, Mr. Acheson?"

Acheson: "Yes, it was just the two of us."

Born: "Now, I know it was a long time ago, and it is hard to remember things accurately from so long ago, but do you remember that Slade Webb, the sales manager for Pure Fision, accompanied Mr. Hardy and had dinner with the two of you? And I will tell you that both Mr.

Hardy and Mr. Webb will be testifying to that effect. Do you remember Mr. Webb being present throughout the time you and Mr. Hardy were having dinner?"

Acheson: "I didn't remember it that way, but I wouldn't dispute it. It could have been."

Born: "Was the talk at the dinner that evening ten years ago mainly about family and friends and old times and what's new - that sort of social conversation?"

Acheson: "I would say that's true, mostly social conversation."

Born: "Do you contend, though, that at some point the subject of product pricing came up?"

Acheson: "As I remember, it did."

Born: "And how did it come up? Did you bring it up?"

Acheson: "Well, probably, in a general way. I probably laughed and said something like, 'This is a hell of a competitive market, Byron. Hard to make any profit here.' No question it had been very competitive, and we weren't making any money to speak of, and I assumed Pure Fision wasn't, either. I was expecting him to say something like, 'Yeah, it sure is. We ought to do something about it.' But he didn't exactly say that."

Born: "What did Mr. Hardy say?"

Acheson: "As I remember it, he sort of beat around

the bush for a while, agreed it was a competitive market, but didn't offer to do anything about that. I think I let the subject drop and then brought it up again, told him Genretta was getting ready to put out a new price list. I think he said something like, 'Well, that will be interesting.' Then, as I remember, he smiled and sort of winked at me, and I took it he meant he would go along with that and raise his prices also."

Born: "But you are saying he never commented on your reference to a new price list beyond saying 'that would be interesting'?"

Acheson: "And then the subject went back to football or something, and pricing never came up again in the conversation. He could have been smiling in amusement, I guess, and maybe he just blinked his eye. I just took it that he was probably sending me a signal that he would go along with the price increase."

Born: "So, would it be fair to say that your memory of this dinner ten years ago was that you tried to get a commitment out of Mr. Hardy and he never gave you that commitment, other than what you read into a smile and a blink?"

Acheson: "That would be one way of looking at it. But my recollection is at least that he was not negative about it."

Born: "Mr. Acheson, you wouldn't expect him to say,

'No, don't put out any price increases,' would you? That would have been as much price fixing as agreeing to raise prices, wouldn't it?"

Acheson: "Maybe. I don't know."

Born: "Did Genretta actually put out such a list price increase?"

Acheson: "I think we did."

Born: "Did you follow up to see if Pure Fision raised its prices soon after you raised yours?"

Acheson: "I don't remember checking that."

Born: "And then you left Genretta and went with another company within the next six months, right?"

Acheson: "That's right."

Born: "And is it fair to assume that, in your new job with a different company, you never checked back on the Savannah market and the competitive situation there?"

Acheson: "No, I was too busy with a new job. I never looked back. Nor have I seen or talked with Byron since that time."

Born: "From your years in the industry, would you agree that *list* prices don't mean much in this industry, that the real competition takes place in discounting off the list prices?"

Acheson: "That's pretty much true. I have seen situations where competitors both raised their list prices, and then discounted right back to the point where the net price to customers didn't change. But, if you want to raise prices, you've got to start somewhere, and the list price can be a catalyst for getting at least a modest increase in net prices."

Born: "You now live in Miami, don't you, working with one of the major soft drink companies?" After answering affirmatively, Born continued, "I understand you are now under indictment for price fixing in the Miami soft drink market. Am I right?"

Acheson: "That is correct."

Born: "You have pleaded guilty to that indictment, have you not?" Acheson acknowledged that he had pleaded guilty. "But you have not yet been sentenced for that price fixing, have you?" Born asked.

Acheson: "No I have not."

Born: "Has the Government promised to ask the Court for leniency to you if you testified as a Government witness in this case?"

Acheson: "My lawyer is still negotiating with the Government about my sentence. I obviously hope for the most favorable deal I can get."

Born: Mr. Acheson, I hand you a document that

appears to bear your signature, an affidavit made under oath and subject to the penalties of perjury. Did you sign this affidavit?"

Acheson: "Yes, I did sign it. It says I was not aware of any price fixing in the bottled water and energy drink business in the Savannah area."

Born: "And did you provide that sworn affidavit to the Antitrust Division of the Department of Justice?" Acheson answered that he did. "And it was true, wasn't it? You really did not know of any price fixing in Savannah, did you?"

Acheson: "I don't know how to answer that. I couldn't think of anything at the time, but later I remembered the dinner with Byron Hardy, and I felt I had to tell them – the Government lawyers – about it."

Born: "What did the Government lawyers say to you to help you remember? And did you 'remember' it before or after you were under investigation for price fixing in the Miami area?"

Acheson: "It was during the investigation but before my indictment. The Government lawyers were questioning me real hard about what I could remember about Savannah and Miami."

Born: "Did you feel pressured to come up with something, some incident, about Savannah to satisfy the Government lawyers?"

Acheson: "I don't know. I don't know. My whole world was falling apart. I didn't know what to do. They said they had information about Savannah, and they said they knew I had information about things I had not told them. I really did not know anything much, but I hoped the Hardy dinner might satisfy them."

Born: "So that's how the Government lawyers got you to change your sworn testimony?"

A chorus of objections came from the prosecution, saying Born had mischaracterized the situation. Born responded by saying, "I really don't care whether he answers that question or not. I think it is obvious what happened." The Judge told Acheson he did not have to answer.

Born concluded his questioning and the two Government lawyers, after consulting with each other, had only a few questions, as to whether Acheson ever felt threatened by the Justice Department lawyers, and whether Acheson had attempted to amend his earlier affidavit in order to make it more accurate. Acheson said they never threatened him, and he felt the later affidavit made his position complete and more accurate. Born had no further questions.

The prosecution next called a statistician who commented on the timing of list price increases announced by Genretta and Pure Fision, as well as the similarities of the pricing for some of the product packages. Ted Born just asked a few questions directed to whether the statistician had looked at cost increase pressures experienced in common by both Genretta and Pure Fision, and he admitted he had not done so. The prosecution rested, and the defense was ready with its motion for acquittal, based partly on the statute of limitations and partly on the basis that no jury could conclude beyond a reasonable doubt that price fixing had occurred.

Judge Edenton looked closely at the statute of limitations issue. If the conspiracy, if any, was over and done with by the end of 1982, then the statute of limitations would have run, and the Government's case would be a lost cause. However, the Judge felt that, under the case-law, there would have had to be an open and more-or-less notorious public announcement of an end to a conspiracy in order to have an effective termination of it, that mere inactivity would not be sufficient. The Judge also noted that, although Sommer had changed his testimony as to a cessation of conspiracy in a suspicious turnaround, it was for the jury to decide whether to believe his first testimony or the revised testimony. So, he denied a judgment of acquittal relative to the statute of limitations. He also felt that it was the job of the jury to decide whether there was sufficient evidence of conspiracy. One thing that came out clearly from the Judge was his belief that, if there had been any agreement to fix prices at the list price level or discounted real prices, it did not matter whether such agreement had been carried out. So, there would be no quick end to the trial. The defense would have to put on its own evidence.

Just then, Jamie Fletcher leaned over and whispered to Ted. "The bailiff just delivered to me an envelope containing the separation agreement between Sommer and Genretta. I think you are going to be interested in what it says."

CHAPTER EIGHT

THE DEFENSE MAKES ITS CASE

The Judge addressed the Courtroom: "Ladies and Gentlemen, you have heard the evidence of the Government against the defendant Pure Fision. Now it is time to hear evidence from the defendant. At the end of the trial, I will give you a full set of instructions regarding the law. But I will say at this time that you should consider all the evidence presented by both sides, weighing the evidence using your own experience and judgment, to determine whether you believe the defendant is guilty of price-fixing collusion beyond a reasonable doubt. To the defense, call your first witness."

"Your Honor, we call Mr. Byron Hardy," announced Ted Born. Hardy first identified himself as the long-time manager of Pure Fision's Savannah operations. Ted began by asking him the ultimate question: "Mr. Hardy, have you ever been a party to any communication of any kind with an employee or representative of Genretta or any other competitor of Pure Fision concerning any type of coordination or agreement relating to pricing of your company's products?"

Hardy looked straight at the jurors and answered, "Absolutely not."

Born: "Do you have any knowledge that anyone employed by or connected to Pure Fision has ever been a party to any agreement or even any communication relating to product pricing between Pure Fision and any employee or representative of Genretta?"

Hardy: "Not to my knowledge, and I think I would know if anything like that has occurred."

Born: "There has been some testimony that sheets containing proposed or actual list prices were exchanged between Pure Fision and Genretta. Has anything like that occurred to your knowledge?"

Hardy: "No, and it would be pointless anyway."

Born: "Why would it be pointless?"

Hardy: "Because we have a number of good customers who would provide us with Genretta's list prices the day they came out, probably before noon on the day they came out, and I feel sure the same is true of Genretta.

I'm sure they have customers who probably would quickly provide Genretta with our list prices. It would be pointless for us to exchange list prices."

Born: "But in that case, neither company would know in advance whether the other would follow with a similar list price increase, would they?"

Hardy: "No, and it sometimes happens that list prices are sent out and the competition doesn't follow, and in that case the price list might get withdrawn, or else the company that put out the price increase will just discount heavier to get the actual customer's cost competitive with the competition. We all realize that the price that counts with our customers is not the list price, but the discounted price, and it really doesn't much matter what list prices you figure from, you just have to discount enough to get as much of the customers' business as you can, and you hope you can still make a profit, but any profit we've been able to make in this market is very thin, very small. So, the list prices are almost irrelevant, and it wouldn't make sense to coordinate on them."

Born: "A mention was made by Mr. Sommer, in his testimony, about a meeting he says he had with you in a lounge called the Tiger's Den. Do you remember such a meeting and, if so, what do you remember about it?"

Hardy: "I do remember it, because it is the one and only time I have ever sat down with Mr. Sommer. Although I recognized him when I saw him at trade association meetings or just saw him here and there, I really had had virtually no contact with Mr. Sommer, and I had no personal or social relationship with him at all. But we both showed up at a campaign rally in support of the re-election of our incumbent Congressman, and I realized I had locked my keys in my car. We were all standing around, those of us who came to the rally, and it was a pretty good crowd, and I happened to be standing near Mr. Sommer. I mentioned to him and to several others near me that I had locked my keys in my car, and I knew my wife wasn't home at the time to bring me an alternate set of keys. Mr. Sommer said, 'It looks like the rally is about to break up, and I'll be glad to give you a ride home.' I thanked him and accepted the ride. He asked when I expected my wife to get home, because she would have to bring me back with my other set of keys, and I told him I did not expect her to be back for another hour or so, but I could just find plenty to do at the house until she got in. Mr. Sommer then said, 'Why don't we stop at a bar have a drink, since your wife's not going to be home anyway when you get there?' He was driving, and I didn't have any good reason to say 'no,' so I said 'okay,' and he stopped at this place called the Tiger's Den. We went in and each had a drink and had a purely social conversation. Then he drove me home, and I thanked him, and we parted company."

Born: "What was the nature of the social conversation you had with Mr. Sommer in the bar, if you can remember?"

Hardy: "It was almost completely about football. The political rally was around October, just before the November elections that year, and of course the fall college football season was in high gear. It turned out Mr. Sommer was an avid football fan, especially college football - he didn't have much to say about the Pros. In fact, he mentioned that he had played college football at some big college in the Midwest, I think maybe it was Wisconsin. Now, I like and follow college football too, but I'm not in the same league with Mr. Sommer. He knew all the stats and all the current players in the Atlantic Coast Conference and in the Big Ten, maybe the SEC also. He apparently tried to get to as many of the games as he could, and he regaled me with stories about a bunch of recent games, and some older ones. I mostly listened and would occasionally throw in some comment to keep the conversation going, but he did most of the talking."

Born: "Did the subject of price fixing or sharing of pricing information or exchange of price lists, or anything else about pricing of bottled water and energy drinks ever come up?"

Hardy looked at the jurors and emphatically said, "Never! And I cannot understand why Mr. Sommer would suggest otherwise."

Born: "Did you ever have occasion to speak to Mr. Sommer in person or by telephone on any subject?"

Hardy: "Well, there was a time when one of Genretta's

employees got into a literal fight with one of our employees at the store of one of our mutual customers, and I had to talk about that with Mr. Sommer and try to smooth things over. I think the fight had to do with shelf space. The Genretta guy thought he was not getting as much shelf space as he had bargained for, and our guy was in the store stocking the shelves with our products. We also have had a few telephone talks about opposition to a proposed tax the Legislature was considering that would hit soft drinks and might possibly catch us as well. We successfully opposed that. Whatever the occasion, it never had to do with pricing of our products."

Born: "One other thing. You mentioned going to the campaign rally where you saw Mr. Sommer, and I believe you testified that it was around October prior to a November general election. Do you remember what year that was?"

Hardy: "It was in 1982. I am fairly certain it was the mid-term election right after Reagan got elected President in 1980."

Born: "There was some testimony by Mr. Drew Acheson about a dinner you had with him some years ago. Do you remember having dinner with Mr. Acheson here in Savannah at some time in the past?" Hardy answered affirmatively, "How did you come to know Mr. Acheson?"

Hardy: "I knew him from years earlier, when we both

worked together for the same soft drink company. I considered him a good friend, although both of us left that company and went our separate ways, and we essentially lost touch with each other."

Born: "Did you have dinner with him some ten years ago, and if so, how did that come about?"

Hardy: "Yes, we did. He called me up out of the blue, said he was in Savannah for a short visit, that Savannah had become a part of his supervisory territory for Genretta, and he was in town on company business but would love to have dinner and catch up on what had been happening in our lives. He suggested a place that calls itself a club, but it is really just a restaurant in a hotel. I agreed to meet him there but asked if it would be all right to bring along one of our new staff members, Slade Webb, and he said that would be fine. I asked Slade to join us. As I recall, Slade was still camping out in a small apartment about four days a week, and his wife had not yet joined him, as he was moving to Savannah from one of our outlying offices. My reason for asking Mr. Webb was that, realizing Drew was a competitor of ours, even though an old friend, I wanted a witness in case anyone accused us of colluding."

Born: "Tell us what happened at that dinner."

Hardy: "Not much happened at all. We brought each other up to date on our families and our careers, talked a little bit about politics, a little bit about Miami and how he liked living there, and I bragged about what a great place Savannah was. We relived a few old-time memories - just normal social conversation."

Born: "Did the subject of pricing of bottled water or energy drinks come up in the conversation?"

Hardy: "Not one word of it. I didn't mention it. He didn't mention it. I had been afraid he might try to get into that, and I was alert in case he did, but it never came up at all. We all shook hands and he slapped me on the back and said something to the effect that he had enjoyed the dinner and hoped we could do it again someday. Then, Webb and I left and went home. I think Drew was staying in the same hotel where we had dinner, and I guess he went on up to his room. About six months after that, I heard he had left Genretta, and I haven't seen or had any communication with him at all after that dinner."

Born: "Does Pure Fision have a policy relating to price fixing?"

Hardy: "Sure do. We don't do it. Period. And if any of our competitors try it on us, we get up and leave the room. The competition is severe here in Savannah, but we tough it out. No shortcuts. Absolutely no price fixing."

Ted Born completed his examination of Byron Hardy and tendered him for cross-examination by the Government. Jed Fuller had few questions of Hardy, asking him whether he had told Acheson in advance that there was to be no price discussion, to which Hardy answered, "No, even though I thought it possible that Drew might bring up that subject, I thought it might be a bit impolite or presumptuous of me to directly question his motives in asking me to have dinner. So, I took him at face value that he had in mind a kind of old timers' reunion, but I was prepared to terminate the dinner if anything came up about pricing, and Slade Webb would be witness to that. The subject never did come up, and I was glad I had not prejudged his motives, at least not openly." Fuller went into some list price announcements where one or the other of Pure Fision would put out a price list and the other company would then follow with similar prices. Hardy pointed out that there had been cost increases to Pure Fision in plastic bottles and, in the energy drinks, increases in the price of sugar, and he noted that, while many of the prices were similar, or close, not all of them were. He noted that where one was selling a commodity like bottled water, where there were no meaningful quality distinctions, prices would always gravitate to a similar level, because otherwise the one with the higher price would lose business and could not sell the products.

The next witness for the defense was Slade Webb, and Jamie Fletcher took him on as a witness for the defense. Slade strongly denied any price fixing, and then Jamie asked him about the visit Paul Sommer said he made to Slade's apartment to leave a price list. Slade said, "I was sitting here in the Courtroom when Mr. Sommer testified that he came to my apartment with a price list, but I notice he never said he gave it to me or even saw me. He is not even sure he remembers leaving it with my wife. Certainly, I never saw any such price list."

Fletcher: "So, do you live in an apartment or a standalone separate home?"

Webb: "I live in a standalone house. The only time I have lived in an apartment in Savannah was when I first took the job ss sales manager of this territory. I had lived about 75 miles out from Savannah before that time, and I basically commuted into Savannah for about six or eight months until I could find a home I liked and could afford. My children wanted to finish the school year back home also, so I took my time buying a home. But I really needed some place to lay my head when it was not convenient to commute, so I rented an apartment. Sometimes I would sleep there four nights a week, sometimes just two or three times. My wife and family never lived with me in that apartment until we bought a house, and she came up with the children to help us move in. So, my wife was not around for Mr. Sommer to give any price list to, and I wasn't around very much. I am not even sure Mr. Sommer had taken his job here at the time, because this was way back about ten years ago, around the time Byron and I had that dinner with Drew Acheson. So, I am not sure I ever had an apartment in Savannah during any of Mr. Sommer's tenure here as a Genretta manager. What I know for sure is that I never - ever - got any price list from Mr. Sommer, nor have we ever talked about any price list."

Fletcher: "Is it possible Mr. Sommer somehow got hold of the address of your old apartment and, not knowing you no longer lived there, slipped a price list under the door of a later resident of that apartment?"

Webb: "If he is being halfway truthful, I guess it is possible Mr. Sommer got my old obsolete apartment address and stuck something under the door, thinking I still lived there. I don't know. But I know I never saw it and have no knowledge whatsoever of any such incident."

Fletcher: "You also heard the testimony of Mr. Acheson about the dinner with Mr. Hardy. Were you present at that dinner?"

Webb: "Mr. Hardy asked me to go with him to the dinner and of course I went. Good meal, but I just sat there mostly silent while Byron and Drew talked old times."

Fletcher: "Was there ever any mention of pricing of bottled water or energy drinks, or anything of the kind?"

Webb: "No, nothing like that at all. Just social, old times and stuff. Pretty boring to me. But the dinner was good."

Fletcher: "Are you aware of or have you heard of any price communications or coordination between Pure Fision and Genretta?"

Webb: "No."

Fletcher: "If there had been any pricing collusion between Pure Fision and Genretta, would you as sales manager have heard of or known about it?"

Jed Fuller objected that the question called for speculation, but the Judge overruled the objection. Webb answered, "Of course, I would have known. I was the head of sales. It would have been impossible to carry out any price fixing without my knowledge, because I was at the nerve center of pricing. It could not possibly have happened without my knowledge, and I never heard of anything like that, and it just didn't happen."

On cross-examination, Jed Fuller attempted to get Slade Webb to admit that, in his two grand jury testimonies, he never mentioned the Acheson meeting as a contact with Genretta. Webb said he had forgotten it because Mr. Acheson was an out-of-town visitor and former co-worker with Byron Hardy and the meal was just social, so he had not associated it in his mind as being a meeting with Genretta in any business sense – plus, it had happened some ten years earlier. He also noted that the Government lawyers never asked him about it in the grand jury hearings.

Ted Born called one more witness, Dr. Thomas Conrad, the economist. Conrad's outstanding academic credentials were established, and then he explained he had been employed to examine pricing of bottled water and energy drink pricing in the Savannah area and described the scope of his research. He exhibited and explained charts he had compiled comparing pricing of Genretta and Pure Fision in the marketplace. He explained that, because the relevant products were commodities that could not be differentiated significantly in terms of quality, one would expect, even in a very competitive market, that prices would naturally gravitate to or near a common level for all competitors, which would explain the similarities in much of the pricing. However, the list prices were not always uniformly the same, and generally when prices would go up, it was because of an increase in sugar, plastic, labor, or other factors affecting all members of the industry. He specifically correlated certain of the list price increases to sudden large rises in the price of sugar. Of course, he also emphasized that the list prices were not the prices paid by retailers who bought from Pure Fision and Genretta, but rather the true prices were discounts, the true arena in which competition took place. He showed charts setting out the average discounted prices in Savannah and in a number of other Southeastern and national markets reflecting the fact that prices in the Savannah area were the lowest or nearly the lowest of any other area – both in terms of list pricing and actual discounted pricing.

Born asked, "Dr. Conrad, as an economist who has extensive experience analyzing competitive conditions in markets, did you see any economic indication that any price fixing was occurring in the Savannah area?"

Conrad answered, "No, there is no evidence of price fixing. In fact, all the evidence I was able to find points in exactly the opposite direction, that it was most unlikely any price fixing has occurred in the periods I studied."

On cross examination, Jed Fuller asked Dr. Conrad whether it was possible that there had been collusion but that the collusion just had not been very successfully implemented. Conrad responded, "Competitors do not conspire, especially over long periods of time as we have here, and then fail to act on their conspiracy. I see no objective indication of conspiracy."

Fuller followed up, "But, Dr. Conrad, you have not been present here in the Courtroom to hear the testimony of whether there were actual conspiracies agreed upon, have you?"

Conrad answered, "While I have not been in the courtroom to hear all the testimony, as a part of my due diligence in my studies, I interviewed employees of Pure Fision and have seen other evidence, and I have neither seen nor heard anything that would suggest any collusive meetings amounting to price fixing. The economic evidence is highly reliable evidence that any such collusion was most unlikely."

The Government had no further witnesses, and the evidentiary part of the trial was over. It was time for closing arguments, and the Government was first up. Jed Fuller went to the lectern and spoke to the jury. He contended there was plenty of evidence of guilt. "We presented three major fact witnesses, and an expert statistician. In conspiracy cases, it can sometimes be hard to prove guilt by direct evidence because the conspirators have every reason to conceal the conspiracy, and they are the only ones with direct evidence. Sometimes, we have to rely on circumstantial evidence. But in this case, we have direct evidence. One of our main witnesses was Mr. Paul Sommer. He was a part of the conspiracy. He was there when it was all happening. He has no reason to lie about any of it. After all, he lost his job over it –"

Ted Born was on his feet immediately. "I object to counsel's statement that Mr. Sommer lost his job because of conspiracy. There was never any evidence in the record to substantiate that statement, and in fact we know it is not true." The Judge looked at Jed Fuller and said, "I don't recall any testimony about Mr. Sommer losing his job over any conspiracy. Counsel is instructed to confine his argument to matters that are in the record. The jury is instructed to disregard that statement." Fuller looked sheepish and said, "I apologize, Your Honor, I misspoke." Fuller appeared shaken and hesitant as he continued, going through each witness one-by-one, and then he concluded by asking the jury to consider the evidence and return a guilty verdict. The Judge then nodded to Ted Born to make his argument.

Born said, "Your Honor before I begin, may we approach the Bench for a side bar?" The Court nodded affirmatively, and Born and Fuller stepped up to the bench for a whispered conference with the Judge. "Your Honor, we feel that Mr. Fuller's statement to the jury that Mr. Sommer had lost his job on account of the conspiracy being alleged was highly, highly, prejudicial. Even though the Court instructed the jury to disregard the statement because it was not supported by anything in the record, we are very concerned that the jury will think it was a true statement that was excluded only because it wasn't in the record. I have here in my hand a copy of an agreement signed between Mr. Sommer and his employer Genretta that states explicitly that he was NOT fired for any reason related to any antitrust violations. This document was produced to me at the beginning of trial pursuant to a subpoena I issued, and I had it in readiness to introduce into evidence if the Government had tried to show he had been terminated for antitrust violations. But the Government never attempted to do so, and therefore I never made this document an exhibit in trial. But in view of Mr. Fuller's prejudicial statement to the jury, I would request the Court to allow me to disclose this agreement to the jury and argue it to the jury."

Born handed the agreement to the Judge, pointing to the pertinent wording. The Judge looked at Fuller and said, "I'll tell the jury." Fuller apologized, acknowledging again that he had misspoken. "Ladies and Gentlemen, I have just been handed an agreement between Mr Sommer and Genretta specifically stating that he was not fired for any reason having to do with any alleged antitrust conspiracy. I instruct you not to consider in any way, in your deliberations that Mr. Sommer's testimony is especially credible because he was fired over any alleged price fixing. It appears that simply was not the case. Mr. Born, you may proceed."

Born thought to himself, "Coming directly from the Judge, that was really more powerful than anything I could have said about it. Jed Fuller has just earned himself some credibility demerits." To the jury, Born said, "This is a case that never should have been brought, and I will tell you why. The Government's case hinges on three main witnesses, and I want to talk with you about each one of them. And I want to ask you to use your common sense and judgment and experience in deciding whether their testimony is reliable and believable. Let me start with Mr. Acheson. His only testimony has to do with a dinner meeting that happened some ten years or more ago - imagine, ten years ago! It was a dinner *Mr. Acheson* set up under the guise that he just happened to be in town and wanted to renew acquaintance with an old friend, Mr. Hardy, with whom he had worked as co workers for the same company some years earlier. Mr. Hardy took this invitation at face value, like any of us would have, and went to the dinner, but taking someone with him as a witness, as a precaution because he and Mr. Acheson were now no longer co-workers but competitors. In all fairness to Mr. Acheson's memory, ten years is a long time back for your memory to be reliable. Some of us even have trouble remembering what we had for dinner two nights ago. He says he thinks there was some discussion about pricing, but he doesn't seem all that sure about it. One thing he did *not* remember, which is pretty telling, is that there was that third person at that dinner, Mr. Slade Webb. Mr. Acheson just could not accurately remember who was at that dinner, but he wants you to believe he accurately remembers what was discussed. The other two who were at that dinner categorically testified that there was no discussion whatever of pricing, just reminiscing about old times. They were prepared to get up and leave the table if pricing had come up. So, at best, Mr. Acheson has a poor memory of a dinner meeting ten years earlier, and that is reason enough for you to disregard his testimony as being unreliable and not credible. But there is something else important for you to consider: Mr. Acheson is under indictment for collusion in the Miami area, but he is in a position there for the Government to cut him a better deal in sentencing if he will just testify here in Savannah the way the Government wants him to testify. Ladies and gentlemen, when a person faces a possible jail sentence, maybe a harsh one, but who can get off easier if he testifies the Government way, he or she has a strong incentive to do the Government's bidding. Ladies and gentlemen, there is unbelievable pressure to say what the Government wants you to say. So, I suggest to you that there is not only a strong reasonable doubt as to Mr. Acheson's testimony, but indeed the overwhelming weight of the evidence is that his testimony is grossly unreliable, to be charitable about it. In fact, he changed his sworn affidavit under that pressure." Born noticed that an African-American female juror sitting in the middle of the front row of the jury box began gently nodding her head in apparent agreement.

Then Born turned to the testimony of Eric Smith, the local Savannah Sales Manager for Genretta. He pointed out that Smith testified he never knew or had been a part of any conspiracy but said he had been present in Paul Sommer's office and had heard bits and pieces of Sommer's telephone conversations with someone he *assumed* was Pure Fision's Byron Hardy. He said Sommer would say things to him suggesting something mysterious was going on. Born emphasized that it was not credible to imagine there was a conspiracy when Genretta's own sales manager, at the very heart of Genretta's pricing, was not a party to it and had no direct knowledge of it. He never heard what was said on the other side of Sommer's two-way telephone calls, and his testimony, if anything, proved there was no conspiracy.

Next, Born turned to Paul Sommer's testimony. "In reality, Paul Sommer is all the Government has, and it's not much. He claims he went to Slade Webb's home to deliver a so-called price list to Mr. Webb. But Mr. Webb was not at home and Mr. Sommer is not sure whether he slipped it under the door at Mr. Webb's house or left it with his wife. He just doesn't remember. It is not likely he could have left it with the wife, because the Webb family was in the process of moving to Savannah at the time, and Mrs. Webb had not yet joined him full-time. This was something *Sommer* did, not something anyone from Pure Fision did. Mr. Sommer never claims he talked with Mr. Webb about that price list, and apparently, he doesn't even remember how he came to leave it at Mr. Webb's door. Mr. Webb has no recollection of ever seeing such a price list. Ladies and Gentlemen, this is the quality of the Government's case against Pure Fision!" Born noticed that two or three of the jurors were slightly nodding their head now.

Ted Born continued, "The other event the Government tries to build up into something sinister was the time when Mr. Hardy and Mr. Sommer encountered each other at a political rally. Mr. Hardy discovered he had locked his keys in his car and couldn't get in, and Mr. Sommer offered him a ride home, which Mr. Hardy accepted. Then it was Mr. Sommer who wanted to stop en route and get a drink at a place called the Tiger's Den. This was not some planned, prearranged meeting. It was a natural courtesy extended on the spur of the moment to someone who had accidentally locked his keys in his car. Mr. Sommer claims there was some talk about prices that took place. Mr. Hardy says there absolutely was no such talk, absolutely none.

"Now if you have any doubt about whose testimony to believe, I want to remind you of something you saw with your own eyes. I mentioned to you in my opening statement that there is a statute of limitations issue in this case, and the Judge will tell you more about that later, before you go into your deliberations. But there is an issue as to whether anything at all that the Government bases its case on, took place recently enough to be a valid claim. Do you remember that Mr. Sommer testified he received instructions from his national headquarters to cut out any price fixing, and that none took place after that point. Mr. Sommer said that all price communications stopped before the end of 1982, and if anything happened after that time it would be a new beginning. We also established when the Tiger's Den encounter took place, and it and everything else the Government has charged in this case took place earlier than that critical date.

"Well, Mr. Sommer gave his testimony at the end of the day, and it was interrupted to be resumed the following day. Do you remember what happened the next morning? I was about to ask Mr. Sommer a few more questions, and before I could do that, Mr. Sommer said he wanted to correct something he had said the preceding day. He said actually all price talk did *not* stop after the critical time, as he had testified the preceding day; now, he said it just continued on a reduced basis. I asked Mr. Sommer whether he had had an occasion to talk with the Government's lawyer after court adjourned the previous day. And do you remember what he said? He said, 'I don't remember.' I asked him, 'Isn't it true, Mr. Sommer, that you met with the Government lawyers that evening and they told you to come in the next morning and change your testimony, to make it fit their story?' Again, he said, 'I don't remember.' I said, 'Mr. Sommer, you've been testifying about things that happened years ago, all through this trial, and now you say you can't remember whether you met last night or early this morning with the Government lawyers who told you to come in and change your testimony, testimony you swore to, just at the end of the day yesterday?' He still stuck with his 'I don't remember' position. Ladies and gentlemen, with all respect, how could you possibly believe anything this witness said after seeing and hearing that? I don't have to try to convince you that Mr. Sommer is not to be trusted. You saw it with your own eyes. Please notice that he's not being prosecuted by the Government for all the things he claims he participated in with Pure Fision. They let him go free because he's willing to say whatever these Government lawyers want him to say. Once again, you saw it with your own eyes." Ted Born noticed the number of jurors nodding their heads had increased.

"Now, I don't want to belabor this much longer, because I believe you know that Pure Fision is not guilty. There are boxcar loads of reasonable doubts, piled on top of each other. But I just want to remind you briefly of some undisputed facts. Everybody admits that this is a very competitive market as far as bottled water and energy drinks are concerned. Every witness admits that. Every witness also agrees that the real competition does not occur at the level of list prices, but at the level of discounts off the list prices. Not a single witness has said there was ever any collusion at the discount level, where the competition really occurs. You have heard the testimony of Professor Conrad who said the Savannah market was the most competitive market he was able to find, among the many he studied. He said it would make no sense for Pure Fision and Genretta to collude on prices and then fiercely compete with each other. He said the evidence of conspiracy simply is not here. So, Ladies and Gentlemen, the Government's case is based on poor memories of long-ago events that did not happen the way those witnesses said they happened, where the witnesses had every reason to toe the Government's line, even to the extent of being deliberately untruthful – which you witnessed with your own eyes. It's an incredible story the Government is trying to sell, trying to convince you there was collusion in a highly competitive market with rock bottom prices and very thin profit margins. How many reasonable doubts do you need in order to do justice for Pure Fision in this case? Well, the Government gets the last chance to talk to you, and I have said all I am permitted to say. But I trust your good sense and good judgment. I know you have been listening attentively to the witnesses and know which ones looked you straight in the eyes and those who kept their heads down and avoided looking at you. I ask you to render an emphatic verdict of 'Not Guilty' for Pure Fision. Thank you for the careful attention you have given us."

Ted Born was wondering what Jed Fuller would say. He looked unsteady as one who was going through the motions, wanting to get it all over with. He did not seem to refute anything Born had argued. His main point was that there was surely a conspiracy, but it apparently did not work very well. He argued that it was a criminal offence to conspire, and it did not matter whether it was ever carried out. He argued that, even if the conspiracy stopped at some point, there had never been a public disavowal of conspiracy, and so it is presumed to continue. He said his statistician witness provided evidence of conspiracy. He extolled the virtues of the antitrust laws in keeping markets competitive and keeping consumer prices low. He asked that the jury look at all the evidence and to do the right thing by convicting Pure Fision. He appeared to be embarrassed to stand before the Judge after having been caught and dressed down for falsely telling the jury that Mr. Sommer had lost his job because of collusion he said he engaged in with Pure Fision.

After a charge conference with all the lawyers, the Court gave instructions to the jury, and asked the lawyers if they had any exceptions to the instructions. Ted had a few minor ones, and the Court gave supplemental instructions. Overall, Ted was relatively satisfied with the instructions, although he had originally been apprehensive because of the Judge's rulings adverse to Pure Fision on pre-trial motions. "Maybe hearing the evidence mellowed the Judge a little bit," Ted thought. Now it was time for the Jury to retire to the Jury Room for deliberations. Ted sat in his seat for a moment, trying to take in what had just happened, receiving positive comments from Jamie Fletcher and Slade Webb. "We have no idea how long the jury will be out. Let's go down to the concession stand in the basement and get a snack, and we can talk down there. They got up to leave and noticed that the bailiff was headed to the jury room with a tray full of bottled water – Pure Fision bottled water! "Wow," said Ted to Jamie. "I somehow think that's a good omen, but just a positive coincidence, I'm sure."

The trio went down to the concession stand, and Ted got himself a soft drink and a package of cheese crackers, and the others got themselves something. They sat down and began to talk and eat their snacks, and when Ted got his teeth into the second of the four cheese crackers, the bailiff came down the stairs and came quickly to their table, saying, "The jury has a verdict. Please come back to the Courtroom." They all hurried back upstairs, leaving their snacks behind.

When all counsel had gathered in the Courtroom, the Judge told the Marshall to bring in the jury. The jury came in and took their seats. "Does the Jury have a verdict?" the Judge asked. They answered affirmatively. "Then please hand up the verdict form." The Judge looked at and read the form silently and then announced, "The verdict form says, 'We the Jury find the defendant Pure Fision NOT GUILTY.'" The jury was polled, and each juror affirmed that this was his or her verdict. The Judge thanked the members of the jury for their service and discharged them. Jed Fuller came over to Ted and perfunctorily congratulated him, as did his co-counsel, and Ted and Jamie thanked them. Slade Webb threw his arms around Ted, with a bear hug, and then favored Jamie with one as well. The trial was over. The Judge stepped down from the bench and walked back to his Chambers expressionless. Ted called the Pure Fision Office and left word of the win, and also notified his own office.

Ted and Jamie packed their exhibits and files in their car, checked out of their hotel, and headed back to Greenville. Jamie remarked, "Ted, looking back at it, it just doesn't make sense to me that the Government ever indicted Pure Fision. The case was full of holes. We worked hard to win and were afraid we would lose because the Government had a perfect record of winning these cases – until this one. But still, as you told the jury, this case never should have been brought. How do you figure it?"

"I'm not sure I can answer that, but here's what I'm thinking. First, some of the facts did not come out the way Jed Fuller thought. He did not realize that Slade Webb was at the meeting with Acheson and Hardy, and that fact destroyed any value of Acheson's testimony about the meeting ten years ago: first, because there was another eyewitness to back up Hardy's version of the dinner, and second, because the fact Acheson could not remember Webb was there destroyed the credibility, or at least the reliability, of Acheson's total recall of the dinner. Of course, Fuller could have found out this fact if he had only asked Webb about it when Webb testified before the

Grand Jury, but he had been told by Acheson that only he and Hardy were present, so it never occurred to him to question Slade about it. As for Smith, the Genretta sales manager, I don't think he had any value because he knew nothing about any conspiracy, but I guess Fuller thought it might help a little to shore up Paul Sommer's testimony by having Smith testify he heard parts of suspicious telephone calls Sommer had made. But, actually, we got a net benefit out of Smith's testimony because, if Smith as Genretta's sales manager had no direct knowledge of any conspiracy - and he's at the nerve-center of Genretta's pricing - it would be hard to believe there was any such conspiracy. That was just a tactically bad judgment call on the part of Jed Fuller."

"Okay, I see that. But what about Paul Sommer, the star witness?" Jamie asked, scratching his head.

Born answered, "Of course, Paul was a Government witness who was in a position to testify affirmatively that there was a price-fixing conspiracy, but I'm pretty sure he never told Fuller that the Tiger Den encounter came about accidentally and was not a planned meeting. Perhaps more importantly, Fuller could not have anticipated that Sommer would lie on the witness stand about the session he and Sommer undoubtedly had that led to Sommer's awkward attempt to change his sworn testimony. When Sommer said he could not remember whether he had met with Government counsel the night before, his credibility was shot as far as the jury was concerned. And Fuller himself had his own credibility problems when he told the jury Sommer had been fired for his part in the alleged conspiracy, and then had to take it back and be dressed down by the Judge."

"Ted, just between you and me, do you think Paul really was fired because he confessed to price fixing, even though the agreement said otherwise?" Jamie asked.

"It's altogether possible. It could have been that Genretta fired him but said something like this: 'Paul, we have to let you go because we can't condone price fixing, but we know that such a reason for your termination might make it hard for you to get another job, so we are willing to sign an agreement saying you were NOT terminated for anything having to do with price fixing.' But it is also possible that Genretta had other managerial reasons to terminate Paul. Who knows? But having signed the agreement, Paul could never have testified that it wasn't true, and if he had, it would only have hurt his credibility further.

"But the Government's problems went deeper than the missteps at trial. The Government had successfully prosecuted more than 30 of these cases and had either won them all or had gotten plea deals that made the prosecutors look good, and they got cocky and must have thought of this case as one where we would just negotiate a plea agreement like most of the others had. I feel confident that they did not do the due diligence investigation of the objective evidence that would have shown them the competition was fierce and competition was strong. And, let's face it: there are plenty of good and conscientious Government prosecutors out there who won't bring a case against defendants just to further their careers, but every successful prosecution is another feather in their caps, and if the investigation is sloppy and they've been successful on a lot of similar cases, it's easy for them so try for another feather when a judicious analysis would have told them to leave it alone. They can't ignore their careers, and sometimes they get carried away."

"But now it's over," Jamie said. "We can move on, and I can tell you we have new developments in some of our other cases, but that can wait for tomorrow. I am so excited, and at the same time, pleasantly exhausted – even though you are the one who worked the hardest. In my mind, I was standing right by your side every minute, wishing I was up there with you. Thanks for letting me examine one of the witnesses. It made me feel good, and I don't think I messed up too bad."

"You've done a great job, Jamie, not only in the Courtroom, but in helping us get prepared for trial. Good preparation wins cases every bit as much as what happens in the Courtroom. I do hope this monster is behind us, but remember, there can be civil cases filed by private parties after the Government case is over. I don't expect that in this case because we won, but it is possible to get sued in civil actions even though you have won the criminal case. For one thing, the burden of proof is 'beyond-a-reasonable-doubt' in criminal cases, but it takes only a 'preponderance of the evidence' in civil cases, and there is a federal statute that helps civil plaintiffs as well. I don't expect it to happen, but it could."

Ted dropped Jamie off at his home, and he continued on to his own home, entered the garage, brought in his luggage, and Lydia was waiting with a huge hug. "Look at the table, Ted," she said. "Roses!" Ted exclaimed. "Yes, and there is something else in the refrigerator getting cold," Lydia responded. "It's a bottle of wonderful Champagne, finer than any I think I've ever had. They are a present, Ted, from your client Pure Fision!"

"No joke!" Ted grinned. "This is the first time in my whole career a client has sent me roses and Champagne, and I'm glad it wasn't a bottle of Pure Fision water! But I tell you what, I'm ready to do justice to that Champagne." Ted and Lydia celebrated well that night. Word of the win in Savannah traveled fast, as Ted and Jamie were besieged the next day with congratulations from other lawyers in their Firm, as well as by other lawyers around the Country who had been following the bottled water cases. Ted was greeted by one telephone caller, someone Ted had never met, who opened his congratulatory message with the words, "Hail, conquering hero!" It was a bit overboard, but Ted and Jamie savored the good feeling of winning a tough case.

CHAPTER NINE

AFTER THE CELEBRATIONS

Celebrations are nice, but they tend to have a short half-life, not self-sustaining for very long. Ted had work to do that had been largely on hold due to the full concentration on the big criminal trial. One of the more pressing matters involved the new client Anson Fowlkes, whom he had met only briefly as he was in the midst of trial preparation, and he had asked Jamie to confer with Fowlkes to get the gist of what seemed like an urgent matter. Ted called Jamie to his office to get the story. "Hi, Jamie," Ted said. "Are you ready to readjust to civil lawsuits after dealing with those sometimes-bizarre criminal procedures?"

"Sure am, Ted, it's a relief. I found a lot of the criminal stuff kind of weird, like the defense cannot introduce any exhibit in evidence, even on cross-examination, while the prosecution is putting on its case. But that's behind us for now, I guess. As for the new case, here's what I know," Jamie began. "As you probably observed in your brief meeting, Anson Fowlkes is an older man, I'd say about 70, and he lives in Kensaw, where he has a business called AFCO – I guess they are initials taken from Anson Fowlkes Company. This is a wholesale company that supplies products to railroads, foundries, and other businesses. He is the sole owner and President of AFCO, but he had a Vice President named Clyde Enzor who had been with the company for years and had gradually taken over most of the responsibility for running it on a day-to-day basis. Well, Enzor approached Fowlkes one day - out of the blue - and said he was resigning and was going to take a Caribbean cruise. Fowlkes tried to talk him out of leaving, but Enzor wouldn't consider it. So, Enzor left, and the next day three others of AFCO's sales staff left as well, including some of the best ones, with no explanation. At that point, Fowlkes suspected Enzor was going into competition with him and was taking some of AFCO's best employees. He later found out that his suspicions were correct, that Enzor was setting up a competitive business and Enzor's new company was called 'CECO,' for Clyde Enzor Company. Fowlkes obviously is concerned that Enzor will try to capitalize on his contacts with AFCO's customers, as he's had more contacts with customers recently than Fowlkes, while Fowlkes had stepped back and left most of the daily management to

Enzor. Unfortunately for Fowlkes, AFCO did not have any non-compete agreement, or other agreements, with Enzor or any of its employees. But Fowlkes of course feels that these acts of Enzor are underhanded and are going to severely strip business away from AFCO, and he wants to know what, if anything, he can do about it, legally. He has been contacting his customers by telephone and letters, trying to shore up support for retaining their patronage, but they have largely been noncommittal. Do you think he has any legal recourse, or is this just natural competition that you just have to accept and deal with in the marketplace?"

Ted frowned, thoughtfully. "It's a tough one, Jamie. It depends on a lot of facts we don't know right now. Generally, without an employment contract or a restrictive non-compete agreement, an employee can leave employment at any time and go to another job or start a competing business. In this case, though, Enzor was not just any old employee; he was an officer of AFCO and is held to a somewhat higher standard of duty. He can make plans to leave and can even do a certain amount of preparation for leaving. He can probably take with him and use in his new business whatever benefit he has developed over the years from his business contacts and knowledge of the ends and outs of the business. But there are some things he cannot do. He cannot solicit employees in advance to leave and come with him, nor could he solicit existing AFCO customers to switch over to his new company. While he is serving as an AFCO officer, he owes AFCO a duty of total loyalty and cannot take any affirmative steps to do anything to harm AFCO, such as soliciting employees in advance to desert AFCO in favor of his new planned business. Nor can he take with him any copies of any of the records of AFCO, because they are the property of AFCO, unlike information he has in his head. One more thing: He cannot take with him and use against AFCO anything that qualifies as a true protectible trade secret, although you can get into a big fight as to what is a trade secret and whether AFCO has respected and taken reasonable means to protect the confidential nature of any trade secrets. In other words, it is possible for a company to forfeit a trade secret if it carelessly compromises the secret's confidential status so that it becomes public knowledge. But if properly protected, Enzor could not lawfully take or use the trade secret in his new business. Also, if Enzor conspired with others to hurt AFCO, there could be antitrust violations in doing that. I don't think we know enough yet to say whether AFCO has any recourse against Enzor or CECO."

"It looks like we need to set up another meeting with Anson Fowlkes to probe further and see if he knows anything else that would be helpful, or at least point us in the right direction," said Jamie Fletcher.

"Absolutely. That's exactly what we need to do. If we can't help him, or if he can 'out-compete' Enzor in the marketplace, we need to advise him of that and not give him unrealistic expectations about legal remedies,"

Ted cautioned.

Two days later, Ted and Jamie met with Anson Fowlkes in a Firm conference room. After the usual greetings, Ted began questioning Fowlkes, "Anson, we are not sure whether we can help you. You know, the law has a strong policy of encouraging competition, and Enzor's new company adds one more competitor to the mix – plus, you can't make a guy work for you who doesn't want to. But there are some situations where certain types of competition are 'unfair competition,' and maybe we can help if Enzor has crossed the line. So, I want you to tell us everything you know about what happened, including any history of conflict or animosity between you and Clyde Enzor."

"Well, let me start with some new developments," Fowlkes began. "First, I presented each of my existing employees, the ones that did not resign the day after Clyde's resignation, with an employment agreement, containing a non-compete clause, and they all refused to sign it. That tells me something. It tells me they are also going to jump ship at some designated future moment. I would bet you anything that they already have a deal with Clyde to leave me and go over to Clyde just as soon as Clyde feels he can support them on his payroll. In the meantime, they are good spies for Clyde and can update him daily, or more often if they want to, on what my company AFCO is doing, and I'm the stupid guy who's funding their paychecks while they spy on me and try to undermine me from within. There is one employee, Dooney McNab, who was on vacation when Clyde walked out on me, and he comes back into the office on Monday, so I don't know about him, but the others are in cahoots with Clyde. I'm sure of it."

"That's one way to smoke out your remaining employees, to test their loyalty by asking them to sign non-compete agreements. But, of course, their refusal to sign could just possibly mean only that they don't want to tie themselves down, wanting to keep their options open. Isn't that possible?" asked Ted.

"Of course, it's remotely possible, but I don't think so," Fowlkes said.   "I've known these guys a long time, some of them for years, and I have noticed a change in their attitudes and behavior. They aren't friendly any-more, almost hostile at times, I would say. I catch them quietly talking to each other, sometimes snickering. I have to direct them to make customer calls, and when we get orders, the orders are often delayed, and we don't get the confirmations promptly. I'm told deliveries from suppliers are bottlenecked. They rush out at lunch and stay as long as they can before returning, and they leave immediately as soon as they can get away in the after-noons. I'm convinced they are short timers, biding their time until they go over to Clyde. One more thing: I found out Clyde's location, and I checked with the real estate agency handling the leasing, and I found that the lease on Clyde's new facility was entered into more than

three months before Clyde resigned. The agent told me
Clyde had visited him in the company of a man who fits
the description of one of the departed employees. I spoke
with some of the neighboring businesses, and they told me
that a group of men had been coming to the leased site
almost every evening for weeks, and on weekends as well,
doing cleanups, renovation, and other work, trying to get
it ready. So, this was a plan long in the making, in which
Clyde and my other employees worked secretly, behind
my back, to put a knife in my business. Does any of that
make a difference?"

"It does, Clyde. It advances the ball closer to the goal
line, but I am still cautious. You see, it is OK, generally,
for employees who are planning to leave their current
employer and go into competition, to do certain preparatory things, provided they don't go too far. The main
thing I am focused on at this point is that Clyde, as an
officer of AFCO, owed the company a duty of loyalty. It
is possible he could argue that he faithfully worked hard
in your interest up to the day he left. He might say he
never solicited business from your customers until he left.
He's got a tougher time explaining his siphoning off your
employees, but I suppose he – and they – could say Clyde
never solicited them to leave, but when he told them out of
courtesy that he was going to do it, they all begged to let
them come with him. Of course, although you strongly
suspect it, you don't know for sure, at this point, whether
those men who were working on the new lease site were
your employees or a construction crew Clyde had hired.

I'm not trying to be negative, Anson, but I am trying to be careful, because, once you bite off a chunk of litigation, it begins to have a life of its own that is expensive and hard to control. Anything else new? Any signs Clyde took any of your documents with him or copied any?" Ted inquired.

"I checked business licenses at the City Hall, and I found out he took one out and paid the license fee on January 2. That was a couple of weeks before he walked out on me. I guess he did not want to buy a license until after the first of the year. Yeah, that's the way Clyde thinks. Like, he didn't walk out on me until he got his year-end bonus. He was careful not to leave before he got all the money out of me that he could!" Anson bitterly reflected.

"I assume you have documentary evidence of the lease and the business license. Let us have copies of them and anything else that's relevant. But what about your company records? Any indication he copied and took them with him?" Ted asked.

"I feel sure he did, but at this point I can't prove it. The documents all seem to still be there, as far as I can tell. I wish I had had a document counter on the copy machines, that would tell me if an inordinate number of copies had been made, but, unfortunately, I didn't have that. I did notice that the supply of copy paper we usually use was low, and there was a different brand of newly supplied paper there. But I don't know if we could make a case out of that. By the way, should I go ahead and fire these employees who are still with me, or just wait and see them leave?" Anson asked.

"I would wait at least until Dooney McNab gets back on Monday. Find out what he knows, and then we can decide what to do. I hate to see you pay people who are spying on you, but in any litigation, it would make your case look better if they walked out on you rather than your firing them. Now, I am not trying to get personal, but we need to ask you something else. Tell us about your relationship with Clyde over the years, and tell us if there is anything in your background or in your relationship with him that he could argue made it intolerable for him to continue working with you. This is something that could influence a jury, which is why I'm asking," Ted probed.

Anson paused and then said, "As far as my relationship with Clyde is concerned, I have always thought we had a good relationship. I taught him the business, promoted him, steadily increased his pay and thought we got along well together. As far as my background is concerned, I guess I should tell you that I was once an alcoholic and had a pretty bad case of it. But I have sworn off alcohol some seven years ago and haven't had a drop since then. Clyde might testify that on occasions, when I was so deep in an alcohol slump that I really wasn't functional, I sent him to go get me some more bourbon – my preferred alcohol. I am embarrassed about that now and ashamed of it. I shouldn't have tried to get more when I was already drowning in booze, and above all, I shouldn't have sent Clyde to go get it for me – that wasn't part of his job, and I suppose it could be called abusive. But that was many years ago, and it surely couldn't have been a reason for Clyde to leave and go into competition with me now. By the way, I have made abject apologies to Clyde about my pre-reform conduct, and he's told me it was all right, just part of the past we could put behind us. But he could still bring it up, and you should know about it. I can't think of anything else negative about our relationship through the years."

"Anything else that might be negative, even if it didn't involve Fred directly?" Ted asked.

"Well, I have been divorced, then I remarried about ten years ago, and we're still married. Jenna was a great encourager and support for me as I was trying to kick the alcohol demon. I owe my present sobriety in large part to her," Anson divulged.

"Tell me, Anson, is AFCO your sole business, source of income and major asset?" Ted probed further.

"Essentially, yes. I have made investments in different things from time to time, once in an ethanol alcohol business– now I'm having to say that word 'alcohol' again! But the major gasoline suppliers effectively killed that business, smearing it with the term 'gasohol.' I have had some other local business investments; some have had to be closed, one or two hung on, neither making much money nor losing much, what I call 'the walking dead.' But AFCO was a niche business that supplied hardware-type products, and the volume and specialty nature of the items we sell worked for us - but fortunately for us, those items were too much of a specialty for hardware stores to bother with, so we didn't have to compete with them. We've given good service and have made good money with the business. I would say it is responsible for about 90 per cent of my earned income at the present. So, if I lose this business, I will be glad I'm eligible for social security, because this is my major asset, other than some savings I have in the bank."

The conference ended with Ted's admonition to Anson to report any significant developments, while Ted and Jamie were weighing the risks, benefits, and potential costs of a lawsuit.

When Anson Fowlkes had taken his leave, Ted turned to Jamie and asked, "What do you think, Jamie?"

"I think he has a case," Jamie opined. "I wish there was more direct evidence. It is mostly based on circumstantial evidence, although it is at least highly suspicious circumstantial evidence."

"As you know, in our Firm we don't take cases on a contingent fee basis, so our decision whether to handle the case doesn't economically depend on the probability of winning or losing. And yet, Anson is gambling his money, maybe his life savings, on whether he wins or not. We need to be sure to tell him what he needs to hear and not just what he wants to hear. Right now, he wants us to sue, but if he sues and loses, he will be even worse off than today, and he will have buyer's remorse. Take a look at all the new cases from the state Supreme Court and see what kind of comfort we can get from them. It just could be, that he would be better served by fighting this battle in the marketplace than in the Courthouse."

"Will do," Jamie promised.

CHAPTER TEN

A MASSIVE UNEXPECTED DEVELOPMENT

It was on Monday, about a week after the conference with Anson Fowlkes, that Ted's telephone rang. "I have Mr. Fowlkes on the line. He says it's urgent," the secretary said.

"OK. Put it through," Ted instructed.

"Ted, this is Anson, and I hope you have some time. This is important. I came into the office today, and I was confronted by the three 'suspect employees' who had remained on my payroll after Clyde walked out. They told me they were resigning immediately and going to work with Clyde. That was not a big surprise to me. I more or less expected it to happen, although I hoped I was wrong. But I hardly had time to react before the next bombshell dropped. They told me that Clyde's company CECO had been bought out by one of the suppliers of some of my best-selling products – a large national company, with millions, maybe billions in assets, Arsenol. Look, it was bad enough when I thought I was going to have to compete against Clyde Enzor. Now I've got to compete against a behemoth that also was my key supplier. Clyde was my prime employee, and as a result of the position I put him in, he now has better customer and supplier contacts than I have. That was bad enough! But it's impossible for me to compete against the resources of Arsenol. And, besides, I'm not sure I can replace Arsenol as a supplier. They might not sell to me at all or, if they will, they will certainly give priority to Clyde, both in service and price. Looks like AFCO is history!" Anson blurted out, very emotionally.

"Anson, how do you think this came about? Looks a little like Clyde decided he could not stand to take the losses and pay the full payroll, in competition with you, and decided to bailout and sell his company to Arsenol, for probably a nifty upfront profit he could put in his pocket immediately. Or do you think this was the deal all along: Clyde could have agreed in advance to 'deliver' AFCO to Arsenol, for an upfront fee and a lucrative management contract?" Ted asked.

"I don't know, Ted, and frankly I haven't had time to think it through, but it has happened so fast – Clyde has just barely got his doors open, and he's been bought

out. Big companies don't usually act that fast with acquisitions, especially startups. Sounds like it might have
all been prearranged. Clyde probably would not have
told his – my - 'stolen' staff how it happened, because
he wouldn't want to share any of the upfront profit with
them. All he probably had to do was promise everyone
an increase in salary, backed by Arsenol's assets and credit and with assurance of a superior supplier relationship
as well, and that would have been enough to get them to
jump ship. I suspect the salesmen are in the dark about a
lot of the Arsenol deal, and only Clyde and Arsenol really
know what happened," Fowlkes responded.

"One thing this does, from a legal standpoint, is that
it injects a conspiracy theory into the legal analysis, a
conspiracy of Arsenol and Clyde to rip your business away
from you and take it for themselves. There were probably
all kinds of other things Clyde did also, like fraudulently
lying to you, and probably taking your business records
and sharing them with Arsenol in violation of Clyde's
fiduciary duty to you. It smells to high heaven, but we
are just guessing right now. Anson, you need to talk with
your contacts at Arsenol, find out whether they will still
deal with you and, if so, will they give you at least as good
terms as they give CECO. If they won't deal with you, or
if they won't deal with you on fair and reasonable terms,
you could have a 'refusal to deal' cause of action. Of
course, you need to ask Arsenol how the deal with Clyde
came about," Ted advised.

"All right. I'll do that immediately," Anson responded. "By the way, I still have one employee. It turns out that Dooney McNab wasn't in on the deal, probably because Clyde didn't think he could trust Dooney to keep it a secret from me. Also, confidentially between you and me, he's my least productive salesperson, but he's been with me the longest, used to be good but now seems to have lost his spark. Clyde probably just didn't want him. But now, let me contact Arsenol and see where we stand."

Ted was stunned. He had expected this would be a typical case, which he had routinely handled over the years, where key employees leave a company and become a competitor of their former employer, either because they had become dissatisfied or were just looking for improved opportunity. But this one was not typical. First, almost the entire sales staff – the main employees of a company devoted to wholesaling – had walked out en masse, with no warning. That was unusual enough. But having apparently set out to start a new local sales company, not really up and running yet, the whole batch of them were "acquired" by a large national company, that also happened to be an important supplier to AFCO. *That* was really a new twist. And in Kensaw too! Kensaw was a growing town, looking to emerge as a true city, but not a place where one would expect a huge company to get involved in a start-up de novo business, selling not only its own manufactured products but a line of other only loosely related products. There were a lot of unanswered questions as to *why* it happened, *how* it happened and the logic behind it all. And hovering over all else was the realization that Arsenol had the financial resources to fight any lawsuit brought by AFCO.

Anson and his remaining salesperson, Dooney, began calling suppliers and customer to gather any intelligence they could about AFCO's continuing relationship with them. They mostly got nowhere with their efforts. AFCO's contact person at Arsenol had no comment, except to say Arsenol would be willing to continue selling to AFCO but said it would be premature to discuss terms except as orders were placed. The other suppliers were polite but noncommittal, and most customers simply said they would have to see how things developed but that they obviously wanted to buy at the best prices they could get.

While public policy favored and encouraged increased competition, and the addition of an additional competitor in any market would normally be regarded as a positive development, it was looking like the old competitor was about to go out of business, replaced by an arm of a huge company taking the assets of the old competitor. Arsenol, by virtue of its size, would probably be able to maximize its profits at the expense of customers – not a pro-competitive result. Would a lawsuit succeed, and, if it did, would it be too little, too late? Hard choices, no good options for AFCO.

Two days later, Anson Fowlkes came to see Ted and Jamie. "What kind of chance do I have of winning a lawsuit against Arsenol and Clyde? I am at the point where I don't think I have any choice but to sue if I have a shot at winning," Anson inquired.

"First, let me ask you whether you are prepared for possible retaliation in the marketplace by Arsenol against you? If you sue them, you may be asking for warfare in the business arena. Are things so bad that you are willing to risk going out of business altogether? I'm sure you must have considered hiring replacements for the departed salespeople. You might actually have a stronger legal case if you tried your best to make a go of the business and still had to call it quits," Ted said.

"Yes, of course I am going to try. I'm not going to just wring my hands and lock up the shop. But I cannot hire salespeople with the experience and contacts of the ones I've lost, because they don't exist, due to the specialty nature of my business, and I am up against impossible odds. I feel like the sooner we recognize the inevitable and go ahead and get the legal ball rolling, the better off I'll be. If Arsenol gets really tough with me after we bring suit, won't that help us in the lawsuit? In fact, I think it's possible that litigation will cause Arsenol to be more cautious and less predatory toward me," Anson responded.

"Well, in answer to your question as to whether you have a good lawsuit, I think your case is definitely helped by the recent developments of the en masse departure of almost your entire salesforce and then Arsenol's getting into the picture in a big way. Yet, it's not an open-and-shut case. We mainly have circumstantial evidence, and you must remember that the law protects competition, not competitors. Our free-market system assumes there will be winners and losers as competition works its magic. Still, the competition must take place in a fair manner, and unfair competition would cross the line and provides a remedy for you. I have a hunch that there is a lot of fire behind the smoke we can see, and maybe we can find out in discovery what happened behind the scenes that we can't specifically substantiate yet. It's not a sure thing by a long shot, but I'm betting there were breaches of fiduciary duties by Clyde and that Arsenol very likely participated in it and egged it on, or at least was happy to pick up the pieces. We don't have to sue all co-conspirators, and it would not be smart for AFCO to sue Arsenol at this time, because Arsenol is still a key supplier AFCO will likely need. Anyway, we don't need to fight Arsenol with all its resources and firepower unless we find out more than we know now. We can add them later, if necessary, but for now, let's focus on Clyde Enzor and the departing employees. We only hope the evidence will back up our suspicions and validate what the circumstantial evidence is telling us. We also are going to have to ask you for a really good-sized retainer before we could take this on," Ted advised.

"I've got some money, and I am willing to put it on the line," Anson said. "I don't think I have any choice."

Turning to Jamie, Ted said, "Jamie, I want you to give me a draft of a complaint. We can get into Federal Court by including an antitrust conspiracy claim, along with an ancillary claim under state law for unfair competition and breach of fiduciary duty. The Federal Courts have a little more experience with these kinds of cases, and I would feel more comfortable there than in state court."

"I've got my marching orders, Ted. I will get you a draft as soon as I can," Jamie assured him.

A few days later the complaint had been drafted, edited and re-edited, and it was passed by Anson Fowlkes for accuracy and any suggested changes. Anson was satisfied, and the complaint was filed in the U.S. District Court for the District of South Carolina. When the Court Clerk stamped it in and returned a copy to the filing lawyers, Jamie and Ted noticed that the case had been assigned to Judge John Newton. "Hey, Ted, I see Judge Newton has our case, just like in my first trial in the *Balentine* lumber stamping case," said Jamie.

"Yeah, I see," observed Ted. "I like that. I've never had a bad result in his Court. I think he's a good Judge. He can be a little talkative and gets into golf or fishing while you are nervously waiting to make some serious arguments, but that's just his personality. He's a bit homespun, but I think he is a good Judge, wants to do justice. We can tell Anson we are pleased with the Judge we drew."

The defendants Clyde Enzor and CECO hired a law firm, Cowder & Wilcox, to represent both of them, and it appeared they would be representing the other departing employees as well, who would certainly be deposed, even though the employees were not defendants in the case. "That tells me something, Jamie," Ted said. "It means they are taking the position that all actors in the departure scenario are equally innocent and that there is no concern of a conflict of interest. They are going to say all of them are totally clean, and we can expect testimony friendly to Clyde from all of them. Doesn't surprise me too much. It's more economical, and they can always get separate counsel later if necessary."

The defendants filed a motion to dismiss on the ground that, even if everything in the complaint was true, the complaint nevertheless failed to state a claim on which relief could be granted. Ted was not too concerned about the motion. Defendants often file such motions, not really expecting them to be granted, but it gives them more time to put together an answer and get ready for discovery while the Court is dealing with the motion. The motion was set for hearing, and Ted and Jamie appeared for arguments at the Courthouse, accompanied by Anson Fowlkes, while David Slappey and Tom Willard of the Crowder firm appeared for the defendants. As they waited in the Courtroom for the Judge to come in, the Judge's Deputy Courtroom Clerk, Lois Latimer, came into the Courtroom and put some files on the bench, briefly nodding to the two tables of attorneys, then going back into the Judge's Chambers. Anson leaned over and spoke to Ted, "I know that woman, Ted. Her brother has a business in Kensaw, and we've had a couple of unpleasant run-ins with him. What's she doing here?"

"She's Judge Newton's Deputy Courtroom Clerk, sort of his Chief of Staff, takes care of scheduling and getting papers filed with the Clerk's Office, really whatever needs doing in the Courtroom, other than deciding the cases," Ted responded.

"That makes me nervous, Ted. I feel sure she doesn't have a good opinion of me," Anson said with a worried frown. "Her brother and I have had some problems that have not left us as friends."

"Anson, you never know, because Judges are human and are susceptible to influence and unjustified biases like everyone else. All I can say is, in the past he has always been fair and objective," Ted told him as assurance, but inwardly he was troubled by this information.

At that moment, back in Judge Newton's Chambers, Lois Latimer was saying, "Judge, I have placed the files on the bench for you. The court reporter is here, and I think everything is ready. I notice the plaintiff is in the Courtroom, sitting next to his attorney, Ted Born. He's the one I told you about."

"OK, let's go on in," said the Judge. Lois preceded the Judge as they entered the Courtroom, and said, "All rise! The Court of the Honorable Judge John Newton is now in session." The Judge then bade all to be seated, as he took his seat behind the bench. This was a regular motion docket, and there were several cases on the docket, but the Fowlkes case was the only one for which oral argument had been requested. The Judge proceeded to dispose of the other cases, announcing rulings made, and holding a few sidebar conferences. Then, as the Courtroom cleared, he turned to the parties in the *AFCO* case, who had previously taken their places at counsel's tables. The Judge turned to David Slappey and said, "Mr. Slappey, I have your 12(b)(6) motion to dismiss for failure to state a claim on which relief can be granted. What's the thrust of your argument?"

Slappey: "I have several points to argue, Your Honor. First, there is a jurisdictional issue. Federal jurisdiction in this case cannot be premised on diversity of citizenship, because Mr. Fowlkes, AFCO, and Mr. Enzor and CECO are all citizens of South Carolina. So, jurisdiction is entirely based on the existence of a question of Federal law, and in this instance the plaintiffs try to invoke the U.S. antitrust laws, claiming that there has been a two-part conspiracy: a conspiracy among Enzor and the employees to harm competition, and a conspiracy between CECO and Arsenol to injure competition. This is like trying to shoot an ant with an elephant gun. We have here a purely local issue. Also, since there are a number of different products being sold by AFCO and CECO, the relevant market in which to consider the competitive effects is very complicated to define and has not been adequately spelled out in the Complaint. That makes the Federal claim defective, and, without a proper Federal claim, jurisdiction of this Court fails, and all the state law claims should be dismissed as well.

"Second, all that this squabble amounts to is that Clyde Enzor was dissatisfied with his situation as an AFCO employee and decided to improve his financial security by setting up his own business. He had no legal obligation to remain as an AFCO employee: There was no employment agreement between him and AFCO to provide him with job security; there was no non-compete agreement, nor even a confidentiality agreement. There was no impediment to his making this move, and plaintiffs have not alleged any. When Clyde decided to leave, the employees naturally wanted to go with him. Clyde was the only manager they really knew, as he ran the day-to-day business while Mr. Fowlkes was basically an absentee owner. After he left AFCO, Clyde got an opportunity to sell his new business, that he called 'CECO,' and the deal was too good for Clyde to pass up. He would have a higher salary managing the business under Arsenol's ownership, at the same time making a good profit on the sale of CECO, bettering himself on the front end and getting higher pay for the long haul. Your Honor, this is just a local dispute involving an employee – under no contractual restraints – trying to better himself. That's just competition. He was not obligated to remain as an indentured servant of Anson Fowlkes just because Fowlkes wanted him to do that. We have freedom of movement in this nation, and Clyde just exercised his legal rights. The law affirmatively encourages this, and for good reason: There is now an additional competitor in the marketplace, resulting in more competition than previously, and customers benefit from that enhanced competition. We submit the complaint should be dismissed."

Judge Newton: "All right. Let's hear the other side. Mr. Born?"

Born: "May it please the Court. I will not say much about the antitrust claims at this point, because they present complex issues, perhaps require expert testimony not required to be included in the initial pleadings under our 'notice pleading' standards. Indeed, it may well turn out, as a result of discovery, that a *per se* violation of the antitrust laws has occurred not requiring any market analysis. It would not be proper, in our judgment, to deal with the antitrust issues at all at this early stage of the proceedings, prior to any discovery.

"As to the unfair competition and breach of fiduciary duty claims under state law, it will be clear to the Court that this is not a garden variety case of a dissatisfied employee leaving his employer and setting up a competing business. Mr. Enzor was not just an employee of AFCO; he was an *officer* of AFCO and, as such he owed a fiduciary duty to AFCO, at all times when he was on AFCO's payroll, to act only in the best interest of AFCO. He had been entrusted with the primary day-to-day management responsibilities that went with his job. Mr. Fowlkes brought Mr. Enzor into AFCO when he knew nothing about that line of business, taught him all about it, opened the company's books and records to him, introduced him to the Company's suppliers and customers, compensated him well, and promoted him to be the Vice President and, effectively, the chief operating officer of the Company. Mr. Fowlkes had a right to trust him, a right to believe Mr. Enzor was loyal to AFCO while on AFCO's payroll holding the position of a corporate officer. Now, there is a great deal of circumstantial evidence as to what happened in this case, which I will mention. But it should be remembered that Mr. Enzor acted in secret, not disclosing to Mr. Fowlkes what he was doing, and so all the *direct* evidence is in the hands of the conspirators, and any dismissal at this stage, before there has been any discovery, would clearly be premature and unwarranted. For example, an officer of a company has an absolute obligation NOT to solicit employees to leave the company, and thus harm the company, while he is still a highly ranked corporate officer of the company. That would be both unfair competition and a breach of fiduciary duty, which is unlawful, far from fair competition. In this case, three of the employees left immediately with Mr. Enzor when he resigned, strongly suggesting that they had been pre-solicited by Mr. Enzor to walk out, while Enzor still had a fiduciary duty of loyalty to AFCO. Similarly with suppliers and customers: the law does not allow them to be pre-solicited by a departing officer, and the immediate adhesion of virtually all suppliers and customers to Mr. Enzor's company – including Arsenol, that quickly bought CECO, almost before it got started – strongly suggests pre-solicitation as a matter of circumstantial evidence. We believe such illegal pre-solicitation will be established once discovery gets underway. It even appears likely that Mr. Enzor and Arsenol had a pre-agreement that Mr. Enzor would act effectively as an 'agent' for Arsenol to 'deliver' all the essential assets of AFCO to Arsenol, for which Enzor would get a big delivery fee as well as a lucrative long-term management deal. Discovery is needed because all the direct evidence is in the hands of adverse and probably hostile witnesses. With all respect, it would be most premature to even consider dismissal at this point."

David Slappey responded by insisting that the Complaint should have more specificity and that it did not adequately advise the defendants of the full contours of the claims.

Then the Judge spoke. "I've been wondering. Was there any event that either party contends was the precipitating cause of the walkout, either a fight or strong disagreement or even a character trait that might have tended to make Mr. Fowlkes and Mr. Enzor incompatible or feel that they could not continue to get along? Anything like that?"

Ted thought it an unusual question to ask in connection with a preliminary motion to dismiss, before the taking of any evidence. Ted answered, "Not that we are aware of." David Slappey consulted with his partner Tom Willard, and then said, "Nothing in the last year or so that we know of."

The Judge thought a minute and then said, "I have some concerns about this case, but I do think it would be premature to grant a motion to dismiss. I am going to encourage both sides to pursue discovery expeditiously, and we will take another look later. The motion will be denied."

Despite prevailing on the motion to dismiss, Ted was troubled, and Anson Fowlkes was dismayed. As they were walking out the Courtroom door, Anson said, "Ted, that Judge seemed to think it was a close question, and that worries the hell out of me. He seemed to be saying, 'I think the complaint should be dismissed, but the smart thing for me to do is to get rid of it later rather than right now.' Is that what you got out of this?"

"I have to tell you I am concerned about it, but this is not the first time something like this has happened to me. Sometimes you think a Judge has prejudged your case, and then when you get into discovery and the real facts come out, the Judge's attitude changes. We should be wary, on our guard, and all that, but I don't think he has formed any opinion yet that is so firm we can't turn it around. I think he is a good and fair Judge. We just have to do our job." Ted answered.

"'Do you think that Lois Latimer might have poisoned him against us?" Anson probed.

"Anson, anything is possible, I guess, but you have to trust the system. I'm not happy with what I observed today, but I've seen worse, a whole lot worse, when we later ended up winning. Now we need to get to work. Let's get some depositions scheduled. I say we start with some of the individual salespeople. If we start with Enzor, all the others will feel compelled to back up his story, tell it just like he told it."

In the meantime, Dooney McNab had returned to the office from his vacation and professed his total loyalty to Fowlkes and swore he knew nothing about Clyde Enzor's plans to leave. When the second batch of employees left AFCO, leaving only McNab and Fowlkes to conduct the business, Fowlkes hired his first female salesperson, Sally Goodloe, to come in and help shore up the AFCO's sales operations. Sally knew nothing about the business when she came in, and she had no contacts at that time with customers or suppliers, but she was a quick study and energetic and worked hard at catchup.

CHAPTER ELEVEN

THE SCRIPT

Ted and Jamie began taking depositions of the employees. Their stories were all the same, as from a script. They each said they had found out Clyde Enzor was working after hours on an office building. They asked him about it, and he told them confidentially he was going to go into business for himself, but he never asked them to come with him. But they were all so concerned about losing their boss, their leader, that they asked if they could come with him. One by one, Clyde told them they could join him, but ordered them not to tell anyone else about it, certainly not Anson Fowlkes nor Dooney McNab, as Clyde did not want to take Dooney. They all admitted they then began coming to Clyde's new site, after hours, to help him get it ready. Meanwhile, they all said they did their jobs at AFCO conscientiously, trying their best to make sales, right up to the last minute. It turned out Clyde could not take all of the employees at once, as his finances would not allow it, so he took three of them, and told the others to stay put, and do their jobs at AFCO. When the time was ripe, he would try to offer them jobs, but there were no promises they would definitely get jobs, as that would depend on how well the new business did. CECO was Clyde's company, and none of the departing employees ever had any ownership in it. None of them admitted knowing Clyde was in discussions with Arsenol to sell the business. It came as a surprise to them when Clyde told them later that he had agreed to sell. However, Clyde had told them he would still be the manager, that they would all be well paid, and they would all be better off than ever. They all denied having taken any AFCO documents with them or having copied them. They contended the only thing they took with them was the knowledge in their heads.

Ted then took the deposition of Clyde Enzor. Enzor stuck to his story that he was a faithful officer of AFCO until the day he resigned. He admitted working to lease his new office site and to get his new CECO office and warehouse renovated in order to be ready to function as quickly as possible after he would leave AFCO, but he claimed this was just pre-planning and preparation that he had been advised was lawful. He said he had never liked or respected Anson Fowlkes and mentioned his past conduct under the influence of alcohol while acknowledging that such conduct had ceased. Enzor said Fowlkes came around just casually, not really involved in the business, and yet Fowlkes was making money off Enzor's efforts, and Enzor did not like it. He claimed he just wanted to be his own boss and have his own company, and he felt he was free to leave legally and do that. He testified he never copied or took any AFCO records with him, saying he had it all in his head and did not need to do that. He said the employees asked him if they could come, that he never initiated any solicitation, and the same was true of suppliers and customers. He said he let them know he was starting his own business but never asked them, prior to his resignation from AFCO, to become his suppliers or customers.

Yes, Enzor said he told Anson when he left that he was going on a Caribbean cruise and claimed he in fact had planned to do so, but then he began to be afraid he had underestimated his costs and the financial backing he would need, and various events began unfolding so quickly he was unable to go on his cruise. According to Enzor, Arsenol asked him if he needed any funding and he had discussions with Arsenol along those lines, until Arsenol suggested a buyout, with a substantial upfront payment coupled with an employment contract for Enzor to manage CECO, including a very hefty increase over Enzor's compensation at AFCO. Faced with challenges due to Enzor's own questionable financial resources, Arsenol's offer was too good for Enzor to turn down. Enzor produced a contract with Arsenol dated a couple of weeks after Enzor's departure, which seemed consistent with his story. It just seemed to Ted and Jamie that these events had all allegedly happened a little too quickly to ring true. "Big corporations like Arsenol don't move that fast; they have committees that study these matters, and they do economic analyses, with big spreadsheets. Enzor and Arsenol must have been in discussions for some little time before Enzor left AFCO," Ted opined.

"Yes, but what if it's true, Ted," mused Jamie, "does that make our case? If Arsenol got wind that Enzor was setting up his own company and they began having discussions about Arsenol's making an acquisition of that new company, would this be illegal as long as Enzor did not try to get Arsenol to drop AFCO as a customer and deal exclusively with CECO?"

"I think the answer is 'yes,' although you raise a good point," Ted pondered. "But if Arsenol was taking over CECO and supplying CECO, I think it is pretty clear that Arsenol would not be able to continue as a major supplier to AFCO, obviously damaging AFCO. And it would be a violation of Enzor's fiduciary duty as an officer of AFCO to engage in discussions detrimental to the best interests of AFCO. Arsenol also was the largest single supplier to AFCO, so it really hurt. And the hurt goes beyond the business relation between AFCO and Arsenol, because other suppliers and customers would likely be more inclined to buy or sell through CECO, knowing that Arsenol's clout and resources were behind

CECO. To them, AFCO would possibly look like a withered has-been. The more I think about it, the more I think we need to add Arsenol as a defendant. It's true they have deep resources we would have to contend with, but I think we're faced with that reality regardless whether they are technically a defendant, because they now own CECO, which is a defendant. Furthermore, those deep resources mean that they have deep pockets also, from which we could collect a judgment, if we are successful in the lawsuit."

"You're not concerned that they might cut off AFCO as a customer, refuse to supply them anymore, if AFCO sues them?" asked Jamie.

"I think Arsenol's role as a supplier to AFCO is ancient history, and AFCO might as well move on from that. Sure, Arsenol might make a pretense of continuing to supply AFCO, but you can be sure the pricing and the terms would always somehow be unfavorable compared to what Arsenol would do for its own subsidiary CECO. There are always back doors Arsenol can use to inject money into CECO equivalent to heavy discounts, even though, on paper, it would look like CECO and AFCO received the same invoice pricing. The hookup of Arsenol and CECO is really what is causing Fowlkes' biggest damages. Without that factor, AFCO would have a much better chance of fending off CECO, because CECO would likely have been under-capitalized. But Arsenol's entry into the mix greatly altered the odds against AFCO. Yet, before adding Arsenol as a defendant, I think I will give Arsenol's corporate office a call," Ted reasoned.

CHAPTER TWELVE

THE ARSENOL FACTOR

One of Arsenol's inhouse counsel, Darren Arnold, was in conference with Wheeler Iswich, an Arsenol division head. "We've got to look at and do some planning about that lawsuit that's been filed against CECO. AFCO hasn't added Arsenol as a defendant yet and, with a little luck, maybe that won't happen, though I think it's probably inevitable," Arnold observed.

"It's really a shame. We didn't figure it this way," Iswich said. We thought that, at Anson Fowlke's age, he would accept the fact that AFCO has had a good run and would just shut it down, sell his real estate, and ride off into the sunset. From a business standpoint, the way we saw it was like this: Clyde Enzor was hellbent on leaving anyway – no way we could stop that. We figured that, even if Clyde didn't leave, AFCO was nearing the end of its effective life, because Anson was going to retire or just let the business attenuate from lack of attention. On the other hand, there was Clyde, some twenty years younger, who knew the business, had all the contacts with suppliers and customers, and raring to be the head guy in his own shop. We needed a good and reliable outlet for our products for the future, so who were we going to cast our lot with – an absentee geriatric, or an on-the-job tuned-in experienced guy with a future? The problem was, when Clyde began to do the numbers, he didn't have the capital he needed, and he was afraid to go into a lot of debt. So, we agreed to give Clyde what he wanted, full control, so it would be the equivalent of his owning the business without having to worry about meeting payroll. He would get paid generously for putting the new company CECO together, and then he would get a good raise as well. What we at Arsenol got was retention of our outlet for goods, plus the capability down the road of making management decisions as Clyde aged, securing our present market and assuring us that we could ultimately control our destiny. Of course, we tied Clyde and the other salespeople up with employment and non-compete agreements that Anson Fowlkes – old fool – had never bothered with. We weren't going to fall into that trap like Anson did."

"But we've bought a lawsuit. In fact, we've bought the lawsuit whether we ever get named as a defendant party or not. These lawsuits can be expensive, and they can divert our attention away from the job of running the business. Also, it means we need to walk gingerly through the high grass of the other unaffiliated suppliers to CECO, without getting into antitrust conspiracy problems. At a minimum, you can expect there will be depositions of Arsenol staff, almost certainly including you. There does seem to be one thing working in our favor. The Judge seems to like our case and seems skeptical of AFCO's case. Maybe we can get rid of the litigation at an early stage," Arnold counseled. "Meanwhile, what position do we take as to whether we will continue selling to AFCO?"

"Much as I hate it, I think we have to say we will continue. Hopefully, AFCO won't be making many sales or needing our products, and time may solve that problem for us," Iswich replied.

Just then, the telephone rang. Arnold's secretary said she had an attorney named Ted Born on the line. Arnold winked at Iswich and said he would take the call. "Mr. Arnold, this is Ted Born speaking. We haven't met, but I am one of the attorneys representing AFCO in litigation against CECO and Clyde Enzor, and I just wanted to introduce myself to you and ask you a few questions. Just speaking counsel-to-counsel, I wanted to get your version of how Arsenol got into this matter and ended up owning CECO. Arsenol has been a long-time supplier to AFCO, and AFCO is concerned that Arsenol would financially back a group of its former employees who we believe engaged in unfair competition with AFCO.

I would appreciate your perspective on how this came about and how you see the future relationship between Arsenol and AFCO."

"Mr. Born, I cannot comment on the events that have transpired up to now respecting Arsenol, AFCO and CECO. I can only say that as a manufacturer and distributor, often through other intermediaries, Arsenol expects to honor its relationships with its downstream distributors and continue to treat them fairly," Arnold responded.

"I appreciate those comments, Mr. Arnold. Could you say whether Arsenol representatives were engaged in discussions with Clyde Enzor about his plans to leave AFCO before he resigned from AFCO?" Born inquired.

"I am afraid I cannot comment on that. Mr. Fowlkes is free to talk with his regular contacts at Arsenol concerning the placement of future orders. Please extend our good wishes to Mr. Fowlkes," Arnold replied. The telephone communication ended. Arnold looked at Iswich and said, "Wheeler, I am expecting the 'other shoe' to drop shortly. I'm guessing Arsenol is going to find itself becoming a defendant in the CECO lawsuit within a few days. Ted Born was obviously fishing for information that would tie Arsenol to Clyde Enzor's departure before Clyde left, some sort of conspiracy theory, I guess."

Back in Ted's office, he and Jamie looked at each other. "Well, Jamie, I heard what I expected to hear – a non-answer. I got a 'no comment' response when I asked whether Arsenol had been negotiating with Clyde Enzor before Enzor resigned from AFCO. But sometimes a non-answer speaks volumes. I am confident now that Arsenol was engaging with Clyde about making a deal before Clyde resigned. Otherwise, Mr. Arnold would have defended the legality of the way the deal came about; he would have frankly told me that Arsenol knew nothing of Clyde's plans before Clyde resigned but began talking with him only after he had left AFCO. He would have strongly defended the legality of what transpired and would have tried to talk me out of adding Arsenol as a defendant. The fact he didn't do that is what tells me Arsenol was in bed with Clyde, possibly encouraging him, while Clyde was still an officer of AFCO. Let's prepare and file an amended complaint that adds Arsenol as a defendant, and we can start taking some depositions of their employees."

The amendments were filed, and depositions began. Arsenol deponents admitted they had talked with Clyde Enzor before he left AFCO, but only after Clyde made it clear he had made an irrevocable decision to leave. They claimed they had not initiated making a deal with Clyde, but that Clyde had sought Arsenol out, seeking financial backing. Arsenol strongly denied encouraging Clyde to leave and at one point had explored with him whether he should stay, but those discussions went nowhere, as Clyde was determined to go. Arsenol had outlined a possible deal with Clyde before Clyde left, but nothing was finalized until after he had left. Arsenol painted the picture of a company caught by surprise in circumstances, not of its making, but acting defensively to protect its interests as best it could. They acknowledged, however, that Clyde had pledged them to secrecy, and so they did not disclose to AFCO that they were negotiating a deal with an AFCO officer who was secretly acting against the interests of AFCO. This, in Born's mind, made Arsenol an accomplice in Clyde Enzor's breach of his fiduciary duty to AFCO. Born and Fletcher also suspected that other suppliers and possibly some customers had also had pre-resignation negotiations with Enzor.

Meanwhile, Ted and Jamie continued to have discussions with Anson about how he was combatting this competitive onslaught in the marketplace. It appeared that AFCO was not doing very well. Anson tried to get a substitute supplier to replace Arsenol, his largest single supplier by dollar volume, and the options were inferior in quality and service. Anson was forced to try to get product from Arsenol, but he was confronted with price, quantity and delivery issues that put him at a competitive disadvantage to CECO. When AFCO experienced a severe drop-off in sales, so that he could no longer order larger quantities of replacement inventory, his old suppliers, who had said they would continue to service him, lost interest in his business, and he no longer got favorable prices from them. Anson actively involved himself in sales, and Dooney McNab and Sally Goodloe worked feverishly to develop business, but business kept sliding. Ted got his favorite economist, Professor Thomas Conrad, to begin working on the magnitude of damages AFCO had incurred.

CHAPTER THIRTEEN

A TRIAL IN SPRING

The parties proceeded with their mutual discovery in which Clyde Enzor and the departed former AFCO employees stuck rigidly to their contentions that they had done nothing wrong, that they did nothing regarding competition with AFCO beyond mere permissible preparation – no solicitation of suppliers or customers to leave AFCO, no solicitation of employees to leave (contending the employees begged to go with Enzor when they heard he was setting up his own shop), and no copying of AFCO records. The leasing of office and warehouse space and renovating it to be ready to go when the time of departure arrived, was all just permissible preparation, they contended. And the defendants further contended that, while there were general discussions with Arsenol before

Enzor left, the discussions were mainly about financing, and there was no discussion about Arsenol's ceasing to be a supplier to AFCO. There were no non-compete agreements in place, and therefore Clyde and the other employees were free to leave at any time and compete with AFCO. Competition is good for consumers and the economy and should be encouraged, not discouraged, they contended.

AFCO's position was that the circumstantial evidence was so compelling that the jury had the right to find the defendants were not being truthful, that Clyde Enzor made a deal with Arsenol to take advantage of his position as Vice President and manager of AFCO to appropriate and "deliver" AFCO's essential operating assets to Arsenol for a handsome profit and to secure for himself a substantial ongoing compensation package for the future, all at AFCO's expense. It was true that AFCO and Arsenol denied they had concocted such a scheme, but of course they would deny it, and all the direct evidence was in the hands of the defendants. But the apparent speed with which the new business CECO was created and then quickly delivered to Arsenol – so unlike the deliberate manner in which corporate acquisitions usually take place – strongly suggested that the whole chain of events had been carefully orchestrated long in advance through a conspiracy to destroy AFCO, taking advantage of Enzor's breach of his fiduciary duty to AFCO during his employment with AFCO.

Some notable things happened during the trial. Most obviously, at every break in the trial, the Deputy Courtroom Clerk, Lois Latimer, seemed to visit with the lawyers for the defendants, almost as if she was a part of their team. Sometimes, she and defense counsel would smile and chuckle among themselves, very unnerving to Anson Fowlkes, who knew there was bad blood between him and Ms. Latimer's brother. Ted and Jamie also began to wonder about Latimer's chumminess with defense counsel, especially since she rarely reciprocated with AFCO's counsel. Of course, there was nothing Ted could do about this unseemly conduct, as there was no proof anything improper had in fact occurred.

There was another surprise that occurred in the trial. When Anson was being cross-examined by defense counsel, he was asked: "Did your first wife have any financial interest in AFCO?" The answer was "no." Then he was asked, "Did your second wife have any financial interest in AFCO?" And then the same question was asked about Anson's third and fourth wives, at which point Ted vigorously objected, pointing out that there was no purpose in these questions except to prejudice the jury against Fowlkes, by getting across the fact that he had had multiple marriages and divorces. The Judge hesitated, but then he sustained the objection to that line of questioning. In fact, Ted had no idea Anson had been married and divorced so many times, and wryly made a note to himself, "From now on, I guess I'm going to have to ask every new client how many times they've been married and divorced. I certainly missed the boat on this one!" At the next break, Ted asked Anson how many wives he had had, and it turned out the answer was *six*. Of course, the early marriages all took place before Anson reformed. His marriage to his sixth and final wife had lasted nearly ten years and was still going well. Of course, the defendants tried to prejudice the jury against Anson by inquiring about his one-time alcohol problem, although Ted had anticipated that one and had already made known to the jury his long record of sobriety in recent years.

At the conclusion of AFCO's case, the defense counsel made a motion for a directed verdict, contending that the evidence was not sufficient to prove liability on the part of the defendants and that the defendants were entitled to entry of a judgment in their favor as a matter of law. Defense counsel almost invariably file such motions when the plaintiff side has concluded the presentation of its evidence, and the motions are rarely granted, so Ted was not particularly worried about the motion. After the lawyers on both sides argued the motion, with the Judge listening but asking no questions, Judge Newton almost immediately announced, "The motion is granted. An opinion will follow." Then he added, as he rose from the bench and moved toward his chamber, "This case has been ruining my spring." Ted was dumbfounded. He thought the case certainly should have been submitted to the jury for its determination, and he was astonished that the Judge would seem to suggest that granting the motion would make his spring more pleasant. His mind then flashed back to the chumminess of the Deputy Courtroom Clerk with defense counsel, and the negative tension between her brother and Anson. "Is it possible that Lois Latimer has been bad-mouthing Anson Fowlkes to Judge Newton, poisoning him against Fowlkes?" No, he could not allow himself to think that way. He had had too many cases before Judge Newton and felt he was a fine and honorable Judge. "Something went wrong here," he thought, "and I have to figure out what, and then turn this result around."

Ted and Jamie went back to their office, accompanied by a despondent client who was beside himself with anger and surprise. "What went wrong?" Anson wanted to know.

"We don't know, Anson. You were there in the Courtroom with us. We thought we put on a good case. I can't think of anything we could have added or done differently. For some reason, the Judge did not think it was enough. He will be writing an opinion explaining how he reached his conclusion, and we will all have a chance to review it and evaluate taking an appeal."

"Yeah, but how long will an appeal take, and how expensive will it be? You, know, I am really hurting. I'm not getting the business I need. I'm trying to keep the doors open for my shop, but it's tough. I'm losing money now, and I don't see any light at the end of the tunnel. I thought this case would be the 'light,' and now my hopes are dashed," Anson said with a mixture of mournfulness and desperation.

"I understand, Anson. I do understand. We are just lawyers, and we can only do so much to influence the timeframes for litigation. I am well aware of the saying that 'Justice delayed is justice denied,' and it's true. We will do everything in our power to turn this around," Ted promised.

"I knew we had a hostile obstacle in Lois Latimer, but now I am afraid we have a hostile Judge. Do you think that behind the door to the Judge's Chambers my lawsuit was decided, not in the Courtroom based on the evidence?" Anson asked.

"I can understand why you would ask that question, but we have no choice but to trust the system. With whatever faults it has, it has been remarkably consistent, in my experience, in producing just results – eventually. It does take time. Justice in the law is not perfect. We will do everything we can, Anson, and if you see how we could do anything better, I sincerely ask you to let us know. We feel for you, and we will move heaven and earth to get justice for you – as fast as we can, though that will be slower than any of us expected," Ted responded.

The post-mortem broke up, and Anson left the office, walking slowly, head down in thought, the picture of abject discouragement and possible defeat. Ted and Jamie shared the discouragement. It had appeared that Anson's

only hope lay in the Court system, and only if he got judicial relief quickly. Now it appeared he might not get relief
in the Courtroom at all, much less quickly. It would be a
long haul if he ever got there. Jamie and a paralegal went
out and interviewed a good sampling of the jurors who
had been sent home without casting a vote. There was
some gratification in the knowledge that the jurors' senti-
ments seemed uniformly in favor of AFCO. "At least we
didn't screw things up with the jury. The only problem
was with the Judge," Jamie thought. Somehow, Ted and
Jamie had not gotten through to him, Jamie rued.

To pour salt in the wounds, word got back to Ted,
through the grapevine of legal secretaries who sometimes
talk to each other on an informal inter-firm basis, that
the defendants and their defense counsel had shared a big
celebratory bash, back-slapping each other and putting
down a cache of good Champagne bottles, with congratulatory toasts for their splendid victory.

In contrast, there were no congratulations for Ted or
Jamie for their hard work, although there were a couple of
lawyers who expressed their sympathy. How could any of
them know the challenges Ted and Jamie had faced, or the
efforts the duo had poured into this case, and the bitter
sting of loss? How could anyone who wasn't there know
that Anson Fowlkes had gotten good representation that
somehow had not produced a win and, in Ted's mind, had
not produced a just result. It did no good to tell himself,
"You can't win them all," or "Sometimes there are days

like that." There was a deep hurt within, that Ted had let a client down, a client who had trusted him and his judgment, and there was no easy or satisfactory fix for it. He could only do what he could do.

As he was searching his mind for a way to deal with his loss, his secretary brought him the morning mail. Among the items she handed him were two that caught his attention. First, there was the promised opinion from Judge Newton explaining his grant of the defendants' motion for a directed verdict. The second was from the United States District Court in Savannah. He opened the opinion from Judge Newton first. It did not surprise Ted. The Court said it rejected the Federal antitrust claims because there was no proof as to what the relevant market was, within which the competitive effects of the alleged offenses could be assessed. Ted had argued that a conspiracy aimed at destroying a specific company did not require proof of a relevant market and, indeed, any such market would be a peculiar one because AFCO had an unusual mix of various products which somehow worked well in the marketplace, even though it would be hard to characterize in traditional market terms. Then the Judge said, as to the state-law based claims of unfair competition, breach of fiduciary duty and common-law conspiracy, there was no direct evidence of wrongdoing and there were plausible reasons supporting the defendants' version of what happened. Now, at least, an appeal could be taken on behalf of AFCO, which could not be done until an opinion and final order had been entered.

Next, Ted opened the second envelope from the Savannah District Court. It was a courtesy copy of a civil complaint that had been filed on behalf of a company known as the "Gas Up Station, Inc.," purporting to be a civil class action lawsuit against both Pure Fision and Genretta based on alleged price fixing in the bottled water and energy drink market in the Savannah area. "I can't believe it! I can't believe it!" Ted told himself. "We won that criminal case, and very handily, too, and I thought surely that would be the end of it. Let me call Jamie."

Jamie came in, and Ted advised him of the two envelopes and their contents. Ted said, "You remember, Jamie, I told you that, when the Justice Department got the indictment and we went to trial in that *Pure Fision* case, the statute of limitations on all civil actions was tolled during the pendency of the criminal action and for a period of one year thereafter. Well, it has been almost a year after we got the acquittal in the criminal case, and here comes this civil treble-damages class action lawsuit based on the same set of facts – they filed it just under the wire. And now it looks like we've got to win it again, in the civil courts this time. This kind of thing almost never happens. You can count on getting these kinds of civil suits when you *lose* a prior criminal case, but when you've won the criminal case – it doesn't happen often. I thought we were done with it. But our victory in the criminal case does not preclude this civil case, partly because this civil action plaintiff was not a party to the criminal case, and also because the burden of proof in the civil case is much lower than the 'beyond-a-reasonable-doubt standard' in the criminal case. Conceivably, a defendant could be acquitted in a criminal action because the jury thought there was a reasonable doubt, but the jury might have gone the other way if it had assessed guilt under a 'preponderance-of-the- evidence' standard. The bottom line is, we are going to have to win this case again on the civil side."

"But our win was so clear," Jamie protested in disbelief. "If the lawyer that filed this class action has looked at the transcript of the criminal trial, he surely would not have filed the suit because he would realize we would have won the criminal case under *any* standard; we would have won it even under a preponderance of the evidence standard."

"Even so, we still have to defend this lawsuit. So, among all the other matters we are dealing with, we will have to take an appeal, and ask for expedited hearing, in the *AFCO* case, and then we have to win the *Pure Fision* case all over again in the civil courts. Here are the papers. Please take a look at them and let's strategize," Ted said.

Jamie Fletcher left the room, reading the papers and shaking his head.

CHAPTER FOURTEEN

THE PROTAGONISTS

In Washington, D.C., attorney Hugh Bigler was talking on the phone with Savannah attorney Schley Jackson. "Schley, did we get that complaint filed in the bottled water case? I've been worried a bit, as we were bumping right up against the deadline," Bigler asked.

"Sure thing, Hugh. Got it done, and I should think service of process would have been effectuated by now. I couldn't get any of the supermarket chains to sign on as plaintiffs, at least not within the timeframe I had to deal with, so I had to settle for my Uncle Jake. He had to close down his gas station awhile back, but he was selling bottled water and energy drinks at his station during the relevant time period, so we should be OK. I'm not much of an antitrust lawyer, so I'm counting on you to carry the ball, but I'm here on the scene locally when you need me," Schley replied.

"Yeah, I can handle the antitrust and class action issues. That's how I make my living. I just watch the CCH reports on Government antitrust indictments, and the plea agreements – that's mostly what happens, the defendants plead guilty – and then I swoop in and find myself a plaintiff and we file a class action treble damage suit, taking advantage of the presumption of guilt that I get out of the Government's success. Usually, the defendants are guilty as hell and have no real defense, so they settle without a big fight, and I get a nice fee. It's easy, low-hanging fruit, you know. These bottling cases have been a bonanza to me. I could retire already, but it's fun and easy, so I keep at it," Bigler said.

"But in this case, there was no plea agreement and no guilty verdict. I guess we don't get any presumption of guilt here, do we?" Jackson asked.

"You're right, Schley, and I had to think about this one, which is why I waited so long – almost too long – to get local counsel in Savannah to work with me. I finally decided I would just be walking away from money if I ignored it. I felt I could give Pure Fision a better deal than I usually give defendants and settle with them for a price they could live with and still make money for myself, that is, for you and me. I'm sure they're guilty – all these bottlers are guilty, and their co-conspirator Genretta says they're guilty. I heard that the Government just plain dropped the ball during the trial. So, I think I ought to be able to wring some money out of Pure Fision. Certainly, Genretta has no defense, as it has already admitted guilt. So, I figured I would give it a try," Bigler explained.

"Have you read the transcript of the criminal trial?" asked Jackson.

"No, if this case doesn't settle and it actually goes to trial, of course I'll read the transcript. But I hope I can make a quick deal that Pure Fision will take because it's less expensive than litigation, and it will keep the publicity down, which is important for Pure Fision. Right now, Pure Fision can tell the world it's innocent, and it has a jury verdict in the criminal case it can wave around to prove it, and the public will either never know about the civil settlement or, in any case, Pure Fision can just say it paid a little money just as nuisance value to move on. Got any thoughts about that?" Bigler asked.

"Not really. And I appreciate your cutting me in on the money. From all I hear, the Government did screw up its case, but I also heard that some of the witnesses got impeached or changed their testimony or something. There's a record of that, which I haven't read either. I know you can clean up a sloppy presentation by Government lawyers, but it's a hell of a lot harder to deal with witnesses that have gone bad. However, maybe we can settle before we ever need to cross that bridge. We'll almost surely get some motions to dismiss or for summary judgment, and we can get a better fix on where we stand at that time, I guess," Jackson said.

Meanwhile, in Greenville, South Carolina, Ted and Jamie were having a discussion of their own. Ted reported, "Yeah, Jamie, we have a puzzled and somewhat angry client who thought the antitrust conspiracy stuff was behind them, and now it comes back to bite them again. You know, even though we won, it was expensive, and it diverted the officers from doing their jobs, and from their viewpoint they won once and should not have to win again. I've talked with Genretta, and they didn't see it coming either. They are more vulnerable than Pure Fision, but this time, unlike in the criminal trial, we are in this thing together, and we as lawyers need to cooperate and develop a good working relationship with Genretta. I have explained everything to our client's management and, even though they are unhappy, they certainly don't fault us as lawyers, and they want to vigorously defend this case, which they think is outrageous. Between you and me, I agree with them it is outrageous. We need to find a way to get rid of this case as soon as possible. We need to get a Dun & Bradstreet report on that Gas Up Station, Inc. outfit."

"OK, Ted. But I'm ahead of you. I've already got a paralegal working to find out whatever we can learn about the Gas Station plaintiff. Sounds like a small mom-and-pop outfit. In the meantime, I'm making a lot of progress on a first draft of our appeal papers in the *AFCO* case. We're possibly a little weak on the antitrust claim, but we think we have a solid case on unfair competition and breach of fiduciary duty, including the complicity of Arsenol in the injury to AFCO. You will be getting a pretty good draft in a couple of days. We should be in position to file our appeal brief early, instead of in the last few days before the deadline, because we know the client wants to expedite the appeal as soon as possible – consistent with our doing a good job, of course," Jamie advised.

"We need to be careful on the jurisdictional issue. If we should lose on the antitrust issue, which is the basis of our Federal Court jurisdiction, that could knock the props out from under our state law unfair competition and fiduciary breach issues. We need to stress the strength of the state law issues and make sure the Court of Appeals understands that we could face statute of limitations problems on those issues if our only alternative is to refile in the state court. But we have to walk gingerly, because we don't want the Appeals Court to think we lack confidence in the antitrust claims."

"Thanks. I'll try to thread that needle as carefully as I can. I know you're occupied with some new case that looks tough," Jamie said.

"Yeah, that's one reason I'm leaning heavily on you in the *AFCO* and *Pure Fision* cases, and I brought in a couple of our other lawyers on this new one. It really gets to me.

Our client is a group of computer programmers who had a non-compete agreement with their former employer, left that company, waited out their one-year non-compete period, developed their own new and better software on their own, and then began to compete with the former employer - whereupon the former employer rushed into state court, got a temporary restraining order, essentially *ex parte*, mind you, and also got an authorization to seize our client's computers and office equipment! Talk about due process! All this happened without our clients' getting a decent hearing in Court! The stuff that was seized contained all sorts of highly personal items in it, like one of our guys said he had a nude picture of his wife on his seized computer. I'm still trying to find out the facts. Our client is telling me they took no trade secrets with them when they left their former company, and they developed their new software from scratch. We'll have to get an independent expert to verify that, but, in the meantime, I'm asking for a hearing to turn around or at least ameliorate the situation. I've got John Mann and Peter Sawyer working with me on that one," Ted responded.

"Interesting! You never seem to be at loss for challenging cases. But it's also interesting that, in this new case you'll be representing the departed employees, just the opposite of what you're doing in the *AFCO* case. Does it bother you to take one side in one case, and the other side in another case?" asked Jamie.

"Not at all. It's not a matter of which side you are

on; it's a matter of whether you feel your side of the case has merit. It's about justice. You work to obtain the best result you can get for your client. In this new case, our clients are basically young people with families and small children, and not a lot of money. They have put their futures and their families' futures on the line for this new business, and now they face a threat that could dash all their hopes and dreams. They feel they did everything right, but they need help, and that's what I'm focused on, to get justice for them," Ted replied.

"And our friend and client Anson Fowlkes is sort of like that, but on the other side. His dreams and his retirement are very much in jeopardy," Jamie mused.

In the meantime, Anson Fowlkes was talking with Dooney McNab and Sally Goodloe. "I appreciate what the two of you are doing, and I know you are working hard. But we aren't getting much business, and not much help or sympathy from suppliers, either. Any ideas? We're hurting real bad," Anson said.

Dooney answered, "I'm getting a little business from long-time customers I've serviced, seems like it's more out of pity than the way it's been in the past – like, 'Dooney's always been nice to us, let's throw him a little business now and then, but it's got to be at the right price,' and the suppliers aren't giving us enough support to provide the 'right price' – we need volume, not little dribbles. I've been thinking we need to find new customers who can use our products in new ways and who aren't that bent on beating down our prices. Take our grinding wheels, for example. We might be able to sell them in a different market. I've got some ideas."

"Well, I'm working hard, too," commented Sally, "but we aren't getting the support from our suppliers that we need, and our customer are all tuned in to the pricing. I'm looking for new markets, too, but they're hard to come by."

"We're eating up my retirement savings, between the business operating losses and the lawyer fees. Maybe I can work out something with the lawyers to cut the expenses. Let's all pull together and try to pull off a miracle," Anson said ruefully.

The next week Anson went to see Ted about the case. Ted had the appeal brief in hand, ready to be filed, and he went over it with Anson, who liked it and urged Ted to file it as soon as possible, which Ted agreed to do. Then Anson turned to a difficult subject, legal fees. "Ted, I appreciate so much what you've done, and I don't have a single complaint about any of your or Jamie's work. I have all kinds of problems with the decision the Judge made to take your well-tried case away from the jury, but that wasn't your fault. I lay it all at the feet of Lois Latimer who I feel may have prejudiced the Judge against me. But I know we can't prove anything – just hope a higher Court will see it more our way. And I don't have any complaint about your fees, except I'm at the point when my ability to pay them is getting tougher and tougher. I'm trying to keep my business going, but that's a severe drain on me right now. Is there any way you can do the remaining work on credit, or something?"

"Anson, I feel for you. You want justice, and you deserve justice, and unfortunately justice costs money. Our Firm normally does not work on a contingent fee basis. We do the best job we can do, on a pay-as-you-go basis, and that's our policy. There are lawyers who earn their fees by taking chances on litigation. It's very risky because winning a lawsuit and collecting a judgment, if you are fortunate enough to get a good judgment, depend on a lot of variables that are not all within the lawyers' control, and you can spend an awful lot of time and effort, and sweat and tears, and end up getting nothing – zilch! That's not the way our Firm operates. We try to do a good job and expect to be paid for it. By the way, the lawyers who take cases on a contingent fee basis take a huge chunk of any recovery that's awarded, at least a third and more often forty or fifty percent. Can you check with a bank or some other source of funding and just keep the case on the cash basis we've been on?" Ted suggested.

"I don't know if that would work. I'm already in hock to the bank to keep the company running. I can try, or maybe I can sell something, some property or one of my other struggling businesses. I'll do what I can, but I would really appreciate consideration of some arrangement, like a contingent fee agreement, giving me credit against it for what I have already paid. I need your services, Ted. I can't - or don't want to - get anyone else involved. I would be happy to pay you cash if I could, but I think it's going to be impossible if this case stretches out very long. Please let's see if we can work something out. In the meantime, I will see if I can raise a little extra money," Anson pleaded.

"That's a fair question. Just bear in mind that I am a part of a Firm, with partners. My partners are expecting me to bring in funds for my work, just as they do, and we share our earnings on a formula basis. So, I am not free to make contingent fee deals without getting the approval of my partners. I will check and we can get back together later. How's that?" Ted replied.

"It's all I can ask, Ted. But please let's do something so you will still be my lawyer. I'll be back in touch." The two shook hands and Anson left. Ted knew there would not be a lot of work to be done in the case until after a ruling of the Court of Appeals. But, in the interim, a decision would have to be made on the financial aspects of the case.

CHAPTER FIFTEEN

NEW TWISTS

Jamie Fletcher knocked and then walked into Ted Born's office with some papers clutched in his hands. "Got something I think you'll be interested to learn."

Ted looked up from what appeared to be a draft of some kind, with penciled edits all over the page he had been working on. "What have you got?" he asked.

"Well, it could be a homerun for us on the new *Pure Fision* civil case. It seems the plaintiff in the case, Gas Up Station, Inc., is a defunct corporation, doesn't legally exist anymore. As I'm sure you know, corporations are required to file reports annually with the state officials, as well as pay their taxes and do some other things. Gas Up was delinquent, hadn't filed anything for several years, and never responded to a series of official notices of delinquencies, accompanied by warnings of consequences. It looks like the company just shut down, closed its doors, and walked away. The premises today where the business was located just house a dilapidated shack and a couple of dusty gas pumps that don't look like they've been in use for a long time. I assume the proprietor just shut down the business and said, 'to heck with the paperwork and filing with the state; I'm out of here!'" Jamie reported.

"Did the State do anything about the delinquencies?" asked Ted.

"I was just getting to that. Here's the kicker: The Georgia Secretary of State has administratively dissolved the corporation. So, the company not only is defunct; it doesn't legally exist at all. Now there is a provision in the Georgia law that permits an administratively dissolved corporation to get reinstated if requested within a certain period of time, but after that grace period expires, the corporation can never be reinstated, *and that period has passed*! The dissolution has become absolute and permanent. It appears that the right of the corporation to sue, and its liability to be sued, is gone forever. Now there's only one plaintiff listed in this case, and if it is incapable of suing or being sued, then there is no plaintiff to support the civil antitrust case against Pure Fision. Therefore, the case is due to collapse and be dismissed for lack of a valid plaintiff to pursue the claims. Yeah, I know, it ought to be dismissed because there is no evidence of any guilt, but that would mean another crazy trial and tons of expense to the client. This is the easiest and quickest way to get justice, as I see it," Jamie continued.

"That's great news, Jamie!" Ted said. "I guess this is good luck we're getting to compensate for the bad luck of having to win this case all over again. I agree with everything you're saying, but then something tells me this is all too simple. What if the Judge tosses out this plaintiff but then grants leave to substitute another plaintiff, a plaintiff that hasn't been dissolved? I'm not sure the Judge could do that, because there would be no valid case anymore that could be held in limbo awaiting a real plaintiff. But the Judge could say it would be in the public interest to allow this to be done, because the statute of limitations would prevent a refiling of the complaint to start a new case. Another approach I guess the Judge could take would be to say that the Gas Up station incurred its damages at a time when it was a duly constituted corporation, and the inheritors of Gas Up's assets should be able to get the benefit of any damages incurred by Gas Up. Maybe I am being too cautious, but this news just seems too good to be true. You did say too much time has passed for Gas Up to get reinstated, didn't you?"

"Definitely," Jamie replied. "I've checked that out, and there are at least a couple of cases which say 'extenuating circumstances' cannot be used as a ground for reinstatement. And, furthermore, no one can inherit anything from the corporation, once the time for reinstatement has expired. Looks like we've got 'em."

"I sure hope so," said Ted. "It just occurred to me we have one other issue that has to be considered. Remember that these rules restricting – or, we think, eliminating – any rights of or through Gas Up, are based on the state law of Georgia. But we are in *Federal* Court, where the operative law is the *Federal* antitrust laws. Would the Federal Court, administering a Federal statute, be bound to apply the state law rules? I think they should be, but I can see how a Federal Judge might say that the vindication of the rights of numerous potential plaintiffs under a critically important policy such as antitrust compliance trumps the state laws and cite the 'public interest' in applying an exception to the apparent rigidity of state law. I think that would be bad law, but I'm not quite ready to break out the Champagne yet. I think we ought to win hands-down, but let's approach the briefing with an appreciation of the arguments the plaintiff lawyers might make. They are going to yell and scream that a dismissal of their case would be a gross miscarriage of justice and that equitable considerations should allow them to move forward with their case."

"OK, I'll get you a draft motion to dismiss and a brief and affidavits to support it, for your review," said Jamie. "By the way, Ted, I'm curious how your case is coming, the one about seized computers, with the picture of the naked wife?"

"It's not quite as grim as it originally looked. I now know more about what happened that led to the seizure order. It seems the plaintiff lawyers in that case rushed into court asking for a drastic seizure order, and the case got assigned to a Judge who was not in her office at the time. So, the plaintiff lawyers in those circumstances were entitled to go hunting for an alternate Judge to hear the motion. They found a Judge they thought might be favorable and took the motion to him. The Judge called our guys and said he had this motion before him, and did our guys have a lawyer who could come quickly to the Courthouse. The truth is that they really didn't have a regular lawyer, but they had used one now and then to look over some contracts and a lease. They got this lawyer to hurry down to the Courthouse for the 'emergency' hearing, and he knew absolutely nothing about the background of any of the issues, and he wasn't even a litigator! So, he was not able to offer anything close to an adequate defense, with the result that this Judge granted the seizure motion, effectively authorizing a raid on the offices of these guys – I call them 'these guys' because they are really a bunch of computer geeks who do a great job in their area of expertise, but they are very loose organizationally. That's when all the computers got seized and taken away, including one with the image of the naked wife in it.

"But remember, this was a quick, substitute Judge that authorized the seizure. When we got in the case and got familiar with the background, we had hopes that the

Judge who was officially assigned to the case might see things differently. Fortunately, our clients had duplicates and backups that did not get seized, so they were able to reconstruct most of their critical business files, but of course there was all the other personal information, including especially banking information and other highly personal information. The plaintiff then rushed in again, blitzkrieg-like, to get a preliminary injunction against our guys to prevent them from competing at all. That would have been the death knell if it had been granted. I got a computer expert to review the new software the plaintiff claimed had been copied and stolen, and on a quick review he was able to say it appeared the software was very different, and he saw no signs of copying. Based on that, the Judge denied the preliminary injunction sought by the plaintiff. She also entered an order that none of the seized data could be seen by any employees of the opposing party, our client's competitor, although its lawyers and expert witnesses could look at the software, subject to a protective order strictly limiting access and disclosure. Of course, the case is far from over, and the plaintiff will do everything in its power to put our guys out of business or bleed them financially through litigation. But the case is looking a lot better now than when we first took it."

"Sounds interesting. Thanks for filling me in, and I hope you'll pass on more of the highlights as the case goes forward. Meanwhile, I'm working on two good ones with you. Let me get to work on that motion and brief," Jamie said.

The motion to dismiss, converted into a motion for summary judgment, was prepared carefully but quickly in the new civil *Pure Fision* case, and at the oral argument, the Judge announced he would grant the motion, and the Ted/Jamie team breathed a sigh of relief. However, the lawyers who filed the case then took an appeal to the Federal Court of Appeals.

While the new *Pure Fision* case was on appeal in the Eleventh Circuit in Atlanta, the Fourth Circuit handed down its decision in the *AFCO* case. It was a somewhat mixed result. The Court affirmed the directed verdict that disposed of the Federal antitrust issues on the technical ground that the relevant market within which to examine the competitive effects of the defendants' conduct had not been adequately established. However, the appellate Court reversed the District Court on its directed verdict relating to the state unfair competition and breach of fiduciary duty claims. Fortunately, the appellate Court also ordered Judge Newton's Court to retain jurisdiction of the state law claims, even though the Federal claims had been eliminated.

Ted Born and Jamie Fletcher had a conference with their client to discuss this development. "Anson, what the Court of Appeals has done is to say that you are entitled to go to trial and have a jury decide your case on the fundamental issues of unfair competition and breach of fiduciary duty. The Court did not approve our antitrust claim, for technical reasons, but that really does not hurt your case too much, provided we can still get to the jury on your core issues. The Court of Appeals has said Judge Newton was wrong to grant the directed verdict on the core issues, and that you are entitled to get your case into the hands of the jury. Since we interviewed the jurors in the earlier trial, which Judge Newton aborted, we know they were on your side and would have likely ruled in your favor, I think you have an excellent chance of getting a good jury verdict when this one gets to the jury. So, all in all, I think you are in a good position. I'm just sorry that justice has been delayed by the directed verdict and the time it took for the appeal to set things straight," Ted summarized.

Anson Fowlkes had a serious look on his face. "I hope you are right, Ted. But time is against me. I don't know how long I can hold together what little is left of my business. I thought we would file the lawsuit, go to trial, get a verdict and then it would be all over, except maybe for an appeal by the opposition after we got our verdict. But time has moved on, and Clyde Enzor and Arsenol have firmly consolidated their hold on my former suppliers and customers, and I am just barely hanging on. Of course, the other thing that worries me is our Judge. He's hostile to me and my case, and of course I think he has been influenced against me by Lois Latimer, who's really got it in for me. I'm afraid he'll still find a way to do me in, even with this appellate decision in my favor."

"Of course, I hope not. I think he is a good and

conscientious Judge who has just made a mistake, as all
Judges do from time to time, and as all of us do. I don't
think he will buck the Fourth Circuit's essential rulings.
But I understand what you say about time not being on
your side. We'll do everything we can to speed things
up. The discovery has basically all been done. We might
need some supplementation and updating, especially on
the quantification of your damages, but that should not
take very long. The main problem is that we in effect have
'gotten out of line' for our trial and we have to get back
in line to schedule a new trial. We will do what we can.
Of course, we can't control the process, and anything is
possible," Ted advised.

"We're in your corner, Anson. We're going to do
everything we can to set things right. We are committed
to that – and to you," Jamie said reassuringly.

The lawyers did some expedited supplemental discovery in the *AFCO* case, and Ted submitted an inquiry to
the Court as to a possible early trial date. That move on
the part of AFCO prompted the defendants Enzor and
Arsenol to file a motion for summary judgment, *again!*
"Ted, how can they do that?" Jamie asked with amaze-
ment. "The defendants base their motion on the same
basic evidence that we've already litigated and on which
the Court of Appeals has determined we are entitled to
trial – and a trial that will go to the jury for decision.
How do they possibly think they can get a summary judgment based on so-called undisputed evidence in the face

of an appellate decision squarely against them?"

"On the face of it, you're right, Jamie. It's hard to see how they can justify a motion for summary judgment when the Fourth Circuit says the case should go to the jury. Of course, they could argue that there are some additional bits of evidence that emerged from the supplemental discovery, or they can just argue the Court of Appeals made a mistake and overlooked something that entitles them to summary judgment, but that is a very long shot. Still, we have to take every pleading seriously and rebut their arguments. This might just be a stalling tactic, designed to postpone the day of accountability, hoping AFCO will go out of business in the meantime. Who knows? All we can do is to combat it, file our brief and prepare for oral argument. We should win this," Ted mused.

CHAPTER SIXTEEN

THE JUDGE ANNOUNCES A DECISION

The lawyers assembled in Judge Newton's Courtroom for arguments on the defendants' motions for summary judgment. Anson Fowlkes was sitting in the viewing section outside the railing where the lawyers had taken their place at the counsel tables, nervously waiting for the proceedings to begin. Lois Latimer came into the Courtroom, put some documents on the bench in front on the Judge's chair. One of the Judge's law clerks came out and sat alone in the jury box. Lois smiled at the defense counsel and then started to move past the plaintiff's counsel on her way back to Chambers. Ted Born nodded to her and broke a slight smile which she faintly and hurriedly returned.

The Judge shortly entered the Courtroom, followed by

Latimer who said, "All rise! The United States District Court is now in session, Honorable John Newton presiding. May God save the United States and this Honorable Court. Please be seated."

Judge Newton announced that he would hear arguments in the case of *AFCO vs. Clyde Enzor, CECO and Arsenol* and nodded to the defense counsel David Slappey to commence arguments, adding, "I have read your briefs and evidentiary submissions, and so you need not belabor the factual details. Just go on into your arguments. I will give each side thirty minutes, and the defense counsel can reserve part of your thirty minutes for rebuttal, if you would like. You are now on the clock, and my Deputy Courtroom Clerk will give you a signal when you have five minutes left. Please proceed."

Ted Born could not decide whether these preliminary statements boded good or ill for his client. Judge Newton was being much more formal about time limits than usual, which could mean he already had a pretty good idea which way he was inclined to rule. But Born was troubled that the Judge seemed to take the motion for summary judgment more seriously than Born thought was warranted.

David Slappey began by saying he did not expect to use his entire time allotment, as he felt the proper disposition of the motion was clear – a troublesome sign, Born thought. "Your Honor, the bottom line is that there is a total lack of evidence that the defendants did anything wrong. Neither Clyde Enzor nor any of the other departing employees were under any contractual constraints. There were no non-compete agreements, no confidentiality agreements, nor any other employment agreements. These persons were 'at will' employees; they were free to leave at any time, with no requirement to give prior notice, and by the same token, they were all subject to being fired without any notice. They had a right to leave and seek to better themselves and make provision for their families. As far as the record shows, they were exemplary and loyal employees up to the time they left. Sure, they helped to paint and refurbish an office in anticipation of leaving, but they did it on their own time, and that is not illegal. You can take preparatory steps of that type as long as you faithfully do your job. There is not one iota of proof that they solicited suppliers or customers before they left, and the testimony of all the employees is to the effect that Clyde Enzor did not solicit or entice any of them to leave; he thought as a courtesy to them that he should let them know he was leaving, and then they all begged to go with him. They copied no corporate records or customer records before they left, just taking with them the knowledge in their heads, which they obviously could not erase and which they were entitled to take with them.

"Now I would like to address the main argument of the plaintiffs. They say the ruling of the Court of Appeals reversing the directed verdict binds this Court as the 'law of the case,' requiring this Court to conduct a pointless trial where it is transparently clear the plaintiffs have no right to relief. We do not agree that the appellate decision should be interpreted in that way. We believe that the most that can be said is that the Court of Appeals focused mainly on the antitrust claims and then left the state law claims for this Court to review once again in an environment not confused with the antitrust issues. There are numerous cases where a panel of the Court of Appeals has ruled one way and then reversed itself in subsequent appeals in the same case. This is not a case where any harm has been done to the rights of anyone else. All that has happened is that, resulting from the departure of these fine people to pursue new opportunities, there is now increased competition in the market, and this is a good thing, definitely in the public interest, as customers now have an additional option for purchasing needs that was not available to them before. We respectfully submit that the motions for summary judgment are due to be granted. Thank you, Your Honor."

Judge Newton nodded to Ted Born to take the podium. "May it please the Court. We come with a very different perspective. We are dealing here with a conspiracy case where naturally all the direct evidence is in the hands of the defendants. They say there is no direct evidence of conspiracy to commit unfair competition and to violate fiduciary duties to AFCO. But it would be virtually impossible to have any *direct* evidence unless one of the conspirators volunteered and confessed his own wrongdoing, obviously unlikely. For that reason, we have relied on powerful circumstantial evidence, which is the only evidence available to us, and the Courts have always acknowledged that, at least in cases where the defendants have every reason to conceal their misconduct, strong circumstantial evidence is completely appropriate, valid, and well-accepted as proof of wrongdoing.

"We start with the undisputed fact that Clyde Enzor was a Vice President and essentially the chief operating officer of AFCO, with a fiduciary duty to do no harm to AFCO but to do his best to advance the best interests of AFCO. It is conceded that he told the employees he was leaving, and it is noteworthy that he certainly was careful NOT to tell his employer he would be leaving. Surely, Enzor had a duty not to withhold from AFCO's ownership a crucially important fact that he shared with AFCO's employees.   He claims that, when he told the employees he was leaving, they all begged him to let them go with him.   He claims he did not solicit them to go, but he pledged them to secrecy and put them to work on his competitive project. The jury was surely entitled to infer that this was an implicit invitation for them to leave AFCO and go with him — the full equivalent of a solici-tation of AFCO's employees to leave AFCO. The same was true of the secret and undisclosed approach Enzor made to AFCO's suppliers and customers. In fact, one of the suppliers financed Enzor's plans and even ended up buying Enzor's planned new business. There's direct evi-dence of those facts. Furthermore, the Court of Appeals, reviewing the evidence on the last appeal, held that the evidence was strong enough to go to the jury. So, it is not merely my opinion that the evidence is sufficient for the jury to render a verdict in AFCO's favor: it is an opinion that the Court of Appeals also shares. Certainly, if the evidence at trial does not support the depositions and affidavits and other proof we have gathered, the Court at that time could say that the evidence was insufficient, but we submit it would be highly premature to grant a motion for summary judgment at this stage, where the evidence fully supports AFCO's claim of wrongdoing and, frankly, we are surprised that the defendants would even seriously proffer such a motion at this stage of the proceedings. There is much else that could be said, but it is all documented in our brief and exhibits in opposition to the summary judgment motion, which we know the Court has already said it has read, so we will not belabor what seems obvious, that the motions are due to be denied. Thank you, Your Honor," Born argued.

David Slappey rose and began to walk to the podium when Judge said, "Mr. Slappey, it will not be necessary for you to make any further argument. I will be granting the summary judgment and will issue my order and opinion in due course. Thank you, gentlemen. Court is adjourned." The Judge gathered his papers and began to leave the Courtroom. Lois Latimer smiled at David Slappey and began to follow the Judge out of the Courtroom. Ted Born and Jamie Fletcher were in unbelieving shock. Anson Fowlkes was drained, sitting with his head bent over, face covered with trembling hands. Ted and Jamie sat there for frozen minutes, looking at each other and at Anson, as the defense team left the Courtroom with a spring in their stride. Ted got up and walked through the swinging gate into the spectators' area of the Courtroom where Anson was sitting. Ted looked at Anson as Anson raised his pale visage, and said, "I wish I could explain it to you, Anson, but I just can't. We were clearly due to prevail on this motion. The Judge will presumably write an opinion explaining why he granted the defense motion, and I will be curious to see what he says. This was a clearly wrong decision. In fact, it flies in the face of the law and in the face of the Court of Appeals' prior ruling on this case. The only consolation I can take is that the decision is so clearly in error that, when we appeal it, I think there is a good chance we'll get a prompt and stern reversal, and maybe even a referral to a different Judge. I just can't understand it. I can't understand it. It is as wrong as I think I have ever seen."

Anson shook his head and said, "Ted, it is not just a matter of being wrong, the delay that would be involved in another appeal is essentially a death sentence for my company. We are on the verge of collapse and folding it all up right now. I don't know what to do. It goes beyond the legalities. Time is my enemy, and this blow might just moot everything as a practical matter, regardless whether we're right or wrong."

Ted said to him the only thing he could say: "Anson, I cannot control everything that happens in a lawsuit. I am a lawyer, not the Judge. But I pledge to you that I will move heaven and earth to get justice for you. That's all I can say. Let's see what the Judge says in his opinion, and we will go from there."

Anson Fowlkes drove home very slowly, almost as if he did not want to get there and face the reality of the improbable event that just occurred. He kept going over the hearing, jumping in his mind from one thing to another as he tried to remember the details of what had happened. But one thing that he kept going back to was Lois Latimer, and the smile she had for the defense counsel at the end of the hearing. "This is all Lois' doing! She hates me, and she's turned the Judge against me. I'm so frustrated, because I can't prove it, but I know it's true! Damn her! Damn her! Damn! Damn! Damn!"

Ted and Jamie trudged back to their office, mostly silently, occasionally saying, "I don't understand it. I can't believe this really happened. And I've always thought Judge Newton was a good Judge. How can this be?" When they got back to their office, Ted said to Jamie, "Well, there is nothing we can do until we get the Judge's Order, and then we will need to do a quick turn-around on filing another appeal. Let's get our legal research all worked up, along with a statement of the facts, and then we'll work as hard and fast as we can to take the appeal. It's pointless to ask the Judge to reconsider. I don't think anything will change his mind."

CHAPTER SEVENTEEN

THE TIME FACTOR

Anson Fowlkes telephoned Ted Born: "Have you gotten an order from the Judge yet?"

"Not yet, Anson. It's only been about a week since the hearing, and it's not unusual that it is taking this long, because Judges are busy. They have a lot on their plate, emergency TRO hearings and other things. To tell the truth, I really did expect to get an order quickly after the hearing, and I even suspected that he possibly had already drafted an opinion before the hearing, but, apparently, he hasn't prepared it yet, or maybe he just isn't satisfied with it and wants to work on it some more before releasing it. I don't know. Presumably, we will get something soon. I'll let you know as soon as I get anything."

It was to be a long wait. For a while, Anson called weekly, only to find that the Judge had not yet entered an order. "Can't you do anything about this, Ted? I'm hurting so bad in my business. I can't go on much longer. Do you think the Judge is deliberately delaying entering an order because he hopes I will just go out of business and drop the whole thing?"

"I don't understand it, Anson. We cannot take an appeal until there is an order to appeal. The fact that he said he was granting the motions is not a basis for filing an appeal, because nothing is official until the Judge signs the order and it is entered in the Court records by the Clerk of the District Court. I have one idea, though. I think I will write a letter to the Judge, with copies to opposing counsel, and politely ask if it would be helpful to the Court for the parties on both sides to submit proposed 'findings of fact and conclusions of law.' Judges often request the parties to do that, because it speeds up the preparation of opinions to have these proposed findings and conclusions already drafted so that they can pick and choose from among them in their own final draft. Let me try that and see if it helps. At least it is a way to nudge Judge Newton politely and remind him that we still don't have the promised order," Ted proposed.

"Okay. Let's try that. I would already be out of business except my two salespersons have developed a new market for us that CECO/Arsenol has not yet discovered. It's an automotive part that seems to have a good application in the mining industry. This will never make up for the business we have lost from our old regular customers, but we hope it will help us hold on a little longer," said Anson.

Ted drafted the letter offering to submit the proposed paperwork, and then he submitted it to the Judge and opposing counsel. Normally, Ted would have checked with opposing counsel first, with the thought of jointly making such an offer to the Judge, but in this case, he knew it would be futile because the opposition benefitted from the delay. A week later, Ted had heard nothing. In talking with Anson, Ted said, "Unfortunately, we have still heard nothing from the Judge, Anson. I think I will call the Judge's law clerk and ask if Judge Newton has received the letter and whether we should begin working on the proposed findings."

"All right, Ted. You know my situation. I'm desperate. Do what you can. I never dreamed I would have run into this kind of a problem. Let me know when you hear something," Anson said resignedly. "Lois Latimer has got to be the problem."

Ted called, and the law clerk acknowledged the Judge had received the letter. He then checked with the Judge and relayed to Ted the message that it would not be necessary to submit any proposed findings. "Judge Newton is real busy right now. He will get to it when he can." Ted thanked him for checking and told him that

AFCO appreciated how busy the Judge was, but that Ted wanted to be helpful, if possible, because the client was hurting financially in the meantime. The law clerk was not responsive.

Time went by. The six month's mark came and went. Ted was getting ever more frequent and despairing calls from Anson, and Ted was exhausting thoughts and ideas to respond to or encourage Anson. He told Anson that, while this delay was unusual, it was not unprecedented. He mentioned that he had heard of several cases where the expected order was not forthcoming for even longer periods of time. This understandably did not comfort Anson, although he realized the delay was not Ted's or Jamie's fault.

Nine months passed, with still no order and no acknowledgment from the Court that an order was in the works or that the *AFCO* case had not been forgotten. Ted met with Jamie: "Here's where we are, Jamie. I have made it a rule of my practice, and have preached it to you and others, that we as lawyers should be deferential to Judges. They are hard-working and usually deserve our trust and respect. Certainly, their high and vital office deserves respect and deference, for there is nothing more critically important to our liberties and, indeed, to our civilization, than a judiciary committed to the just and impartial application of the rule of law. They deserve our patience as well, because patience and unhurried consideration are necessary for just rulings. They also deserve our patience because they are human, as we are, though impressed with heavy responsibilities. We, as lawyers, also are officers of the Courts, and as such we have a special responsibility to understand and defend all Judges as they go about the administration of justice."

Jamie interjected, "I think I am about to hear a 'but' coming. Am I right?"

"Yes, you are right. My 'but' does not qualify anything I have said about deference to the judiciary. It is just that we really have additional obligations and responsibilities which must be accommodated without doing violence to our duty of deference to the judiciary. We have a fiduciary responsibility of loyalty to a client who has put trust in us, to say nothing about paying us, at least in part, for our best efforts. Our client has already incurred two delays which in my opinion resulted from erroneous rulings, and we cannot even get into position to appeal the most recent one – can't even get an official ruling on that one. The client is poised to lose everything if he cannot get the errors corrected on appeal, and yet he is stymied from taking an appeal. The question is: how do we accommodate deference to the judiciary and the fulfillment of our fiduciary obligation to the client?"

"Yeah, that's a tough one. I feel for Anson. At this point it looks like the system has let him down. Do you think his bad results thus far have been caused by Lois Latimer? Do you think she is lurking in the background advocating against AFCO and Anson? If so, maybe such improper influence moderates our duty of deference," Jamie suggested.

"Jamie, I am fighting that demon within me every minute," Ted said. "I simply cannot allow myself to think that way. We have no proof Lois has been improperly influencing the Judge. I have always respected Judge Newton, and I must keep believing in the system. There must be a way, even when we think we have tried everything. I think we need to talk with Judge Frank Tarkenton. He used to be a partner in our law firm before you came with us, Jamie. He was appointed as a U. S. District Judge and served for about ten years before retiring from the bench to take an in-house general counsel position with one of our clients. I think he's now retired from that position as well, although he might be in the process of phasing out and not totally retired. Maybe he could talk to us from the perspective of a Judge and give us some insights as to how we might handle this situation. I'll try to contact him."

The next day, Ted was able to reach Frank Tarkenton. After giving Tarkenton the background of the dilemma he faced, Ted asked Tarkenton for some "fatherly" advice. "Ted, I am not sure what to tell you. I once had a situation where I had put aside a ruling I was supposed to make. It was a complicated matter, and I had a tendency to deal with the easy things first and put off the tough ones. So, it lingered for a while – nowhere near as long as the delay you're experiencing - and one of the lawyers wrote me a polite letter and asked me if I could possibly give them a ruling, emphasizing that he was not asking me to make any certain kind of ruling; he just wanted a ruling of some kind, whatever it might be. I had no problem with this request, and in fact I was sympathetic with the need for resolution. I thanked him for mentioning it, and then I re-focused on the case and got out the ruling. I was not offended, and thought it was a reasonable request. If you do something like that, and politely note the amount of time that has passed, you might find that your Judge would follow through. That's my only suggestion."

Although Born had done something like this earlier, when he had offered to provide proposed findings, he had not yet written the kind of letter Tarkenton had suggested, so he thought it was worth trying. He wrote a letter to the Judge, of course with copies to the opposing counsel, saying essentially that he was mindful of the Judge's busy schedule and was reluctant to write, but the client was incurring heavy losses and he just wished to inquire if an Order of some kind might be forthcoming, whatever it might be. He thanked the Judge for his time and attention and signed it "respectfully, Ted Born, Counsel for Plaintiff AFCO." The Judge did not acknowledge the letter, nor did the Court take any action to file an Order.

Time dragged on, with Born receiving increasingly frantic and desperate calls from Anson Fowlkes. There seemed to be little Born could do to help.

There was a new development, though, in the *Pure Fision* civil case. The Court of Appeals entered an order requesting the Georgia Supreme Court for an opinion based on the State law of Georgia as to whether a dissolution of a corporation, such as Gas Up, would render the former corporation incapable of maintaining a Federal antitrust case for alleged damages incurred while it was still a bona fide corporation. Ted was not happy. He discussed it with Jamie Fletcher. "Jamie, we expected the Court of Appeals to affirm the District Court because it seemed so clear from the wording of the Georgia dissolution statute that a dissolved corporation essentially disappears, for all purposes. Gas Up just doesn't exist as a corporation, or otherwise, in contemplation of the law. And the statute clearly says such a dissolved corporation can neither sue nor be sued after the expiration of the grace period for reinstatement. But now we have to litigate that issue in the Supreme Court of Georgia, and that will delay a final decision in this matter and will add to the client's expenses. Can you figure it?"

Jamie stroked his chin and said, "Not really. The Court should have just thrown the case out. It was only a lawyer-created case designed to enrich the plaintiff lawyers and do no good for anyone else – a case that never should have been brought in the first place. The Court had an easy way to get rid of it, and now we have this extra layer of litigation to deal with. The only thing I can figure is that the Court was aware that, if it dismissed this case, it would be too late for anyone else to file a class action lawsuit because the statute of limitations would bar such a suit, and the Court was sensitive to the strong public interest in antitrust enforcement and was hesitant to dispose of the case without crossing every 'T' and dotting every 'I,'" Jamie guessed.

"Well, things don't seem to be going the way we think they should, either in the *Pure Fision* case or the *AFCO* case," Ted said. "Maybe we aren't using the right kind of deodorant or something. A lawyer ought to be able to win good cases, and we seem to be having trouble doing that – even though I think our cases have strong merit, and we are doing the best lawyering we can do. I still believe in the system, but sometimes I have to try hard to reinforce that conviction."

CHAPTER EIGHTEEN

THE ULTIMATE OPTION

Time continued to move on, but there was no movement from the District Court in the *AFCO* case. Ted
and Jamie had filed their briefs in the *Pure Fision* case in
the Georgia Supreme Court, as had the opposing counsel,
and the parties were awaiting a decision there. So, there
was as yet no resolution in either of those cases. The
date marking the anniversary of the summary judgment
hearing in the A*FCO* case was close at hand.

Ted Born and Jamie Fletcher had another of their
frustrating meetings about the *AFCO* case. Ted had a
particularly serious look on his face. "Jamie, we are ap-
proaching our Rubicon. It has been almost a full twelve
months now that we have been waiting for an order from
Judge Newton. I feel our fiduciary duty to our client

requires us to take an action I have been dreading to take, dreading even to consider taking. Yet, having done everything in my power to get an Order from the Court and having seemingly been ignored while our client suffers horribly, I cannot ask our client to wait any longer. We have a situation where the Judge has heard a lot of evidence in this case from live witnesses and exhibits, and he felt sure enough of himself to order a directed verdict against us. Then we got that reversed, did further discovery, and submitted briefs, and then had oral arguments. The Judge seemed to feel so strongly in his view of the case that he did not even find it necessary to listen to rebuttal arguments the defendants were about to make. We have done everything we could politely do to get the Judge to enter an order that would allow us to appeal. He has refused or ignored every effort we have made – and, indeed, we should not have had to make any overtures to the Judge. His duty was to make his decision and then give us the opportunity to appeal if we wished. I will wait until the first anniversary date has passed before I do anything, still hoping the. Judge, on his own, will enter an order in this case. There is a possibility that he will. The Judges are required to file explanations periodically, explaining why long-pending matters have not been disposed of, and maybe he will want to dispose of this one before it gets twelve months old. But if he does not, then we have to take some kind of action. I remember conversations you and I have had in the past where I have hammered away at the theme that you should always do everything in your power not to get on the wrong side of a Judge, especially an all-powerful, life-tenured Federal judge. That's the way it should be. That is aspirational to the highest degree. But it cannot immobilize us from proper representation of a client to whom we owe a strong fiduciary duty, and when all other alternatives have failed."

Jamie was listening intensely. "So, what are you thinking of doing? We've tried almost everything."

"You probably know what I'm thinking," Ted answered. "There's only one thing left that we *can* do, the only option we have: file a mandamus petition with the Court of Appeals asking it to order Judge Newton to file his summary judgment order. Obviously, this requires the highest level of diplomacy, graciousness, and deference, with no hint of bitterness or rancor, exhibiting only respect for a distinguished Judge. We can wait until the anniversary date passes, but then we need to be ready to act. Are you with me?"

"Whatever you say, Ted. I can't argue with anything you have said, and I don't know of any alternative. This is the whole purpose of writs of mandamus - specifically to compel a lower Court Judge to do what he or she should do anyway. But generally, it applies only to technical, nondiscretionary acts – ministerial acts, as they call them. Can we say this is a ministerial act?" Jamie responded.

"I think it is ministerial. The Judge has already

made his decision and has told us what it was. He just has not put it on paper. That is a ministerial act, in my judgment. Now, I have been thinking, there is one intermediate thing we could do, but I don't think I favor it. We could draft up the motion and hold off on filing it, but we would send a draft to Judge Newton and tell him we will feel compelled to file it if he does not act within a certain number of days. The problem is that this would sound like a threat, and I am concerned that Judge Newton would be more offended by that approach than by our just filing the mandamus petition. In the end, my inclination would be to do things 'by the book,' doing everything via official pleadings, the way the Federal Rules contemplate. It's not good. It's not what I want. But there are no good choices."

The anniversary date came and passed, and Ted and Jamie filed their mandamus petition, using every expression of deference and respect they could think of, beginning with the introductory words, "We have the greatest possible respect for the distinguished District Judge, and file this petition with great reluctance, and only because we feel compelled by our fiduciary responsibility to our client who day-by-day has been incurring unsustainable losses in his business while awaiting for more than a year for an order of the District Court, announced but not entered, to unlock the possibility of an appeal. We have offered to assist the District Court by submitting findings of fact and conclusions and law but were told these would be unnecessary, and we have provided reminders to the

Court of the passage of time to which we have received no response. We are not requesting the District Court to enter any specific disposition in its order, but only to enter some kind of appealable order, whatever it might be."

Judge Newton had an immediate reaction. He directed his law clerk to call Ted Born and tell him that his petition was "received in the spirit in which it was made." Ted, thinking that perhaps the Judge meant he had no ill will on account of the filing, told the law clerk that he had hoped the Court would understand and that the petition had been filed very reluctantly out of necessity for the client, and without any desire to offend Judge Newton, for whom he had always had and still had the greatest respect.

It did not take long for Born and Fletcher to learn what Judge Newton really meant from his message about "receiving in the spirit in which the petition was filed." The Judge did not wait for the Court of Appeals to act on the petition for mandamus. He filed the long-awaited Order granting the defendants' motions for summary judgment, accompanied by a cutting, almost vicious and extreme opinion that excoriated the plaintiff, and implicitly the plaintiff's counsel, far beyond the limits of normal litigation and judicial standards. Ted and Jamie knew then that they had indeed gotten on the "wrong side of a Federal Judge."

The Order and opinion of Judge Newton had no

immediate effect on Ted Born's handling of judicial relations relative to the *AFCO* litigation, because AFCO's appeal he was finally able to file took the case was out of the hands of Judge Newton while the appeal was pending. However, the wider relationship between Judge Newton and Ted Born was heavily impacted. Born had other cases pending before Judge Newton, and Born was apprehensive when appearing before the Judge. He got some rulings on motions in some of the other cases that he suspected were negatively affected by his relationship with the Judge, although he fought the temptation to place the blame on bias. Ted also felt obligated to tell other clients and potential clients who wanted him to handle cases before Judge Newton, that he no longer had a good relationship with the Judge and that their cases might be adversely impacted on that account. Notwithstanding the cautionary warning, none of them opted to have a different lawyer represent them. Ted's relationship with some of his law partners also was cooler than it had been, or at least it seemed so to him. Ted literally had nightmares about the damaged relationship with the Judge. He kept asking himself what he might have done differently and how he might somehow apologize or do something to make amends. Jamie said to him, "Ted, you are much older and wiser than I am, but you have done nothing wrong and have no reason to apologize. I don't think you should." Ted did not apologize, but it was one of the lowest points in his career. Lydia was understanding and comforting, but she also shared in the pain.

Meanwhile, the appeal was pending. Ted had many other matters to deal with, one of them being an appearance before the Supreme Court of Georgia. Ted thought the argument went well, and now he would be awaiting the opinion of that Court, as to whether an irrevocable dissolution was an absolute bar to any claims the former company might have had while it was still viable, specifically an antitrust class action.

In his "naked wife photo" case, the plaintiffs continued to be vicious and relentless in trying to shut down the new competitive business of "our guys," getting the FBI involved in the hope of getting that agency to seek an indictment for criminal trade secret misappropriation. Ted and one of his associates, Paul Sawyer, met with the investigating agents and presented a slide show of documents and evidence refuting the charges. By the end of the conference, the agents were clearly convinced the charges were without merit. Indeed, as they left the conference, they were considering whether to pursue a charge against the accusing plaintiffs for making false statements to the FBI. Meanwhile, the case was proceeding toward trial in the state Court, and it seemed the clients' counterclaim was getting stronger and stronger as discovery proceeded toward conclusion.

Ted continued to field telephone calls from an anxious and increasingly desperate Anson Fowlkes, for which Ted had no good answers except to be patient and trust the system. The Court of Appeals relatively soon issued a ruling on AFCO's appeal, although to Ted Born and Anson Fowlkes, it seemed like an eternity. The Court unanimously reversed Judge Newton's summary judgment ruling and made it clear that the case definitely was due to go to a jury trial. Indeed, the decision was rendered without the necessity of oral argument. Ted suspected that the speed of granting of the reversal possibly also reflected the Fourth Circuit's strong disapproval of the Judge's extraordinary delay in getting out an Order and possibly the animus reflected in his eventual Order. It was a reassuring victory for Ted and Jamie, but it did not resolve the problem that Ted and Jamie still had to deal with in terms of an impaired relationship with Judge Newton.

Ted and Jamie met to assess the situation. "Jamie, we've won a big battle in getting a strong opinion of the Court of Appeals, but we are still going to have to face a Judge who might be more embittered than ever by this implicit rebuke from the Fourth Circuit. We will have to walk very gingerly. I have been concerned ever since the Judge belatedly entered his Order that, if I made one misstep, or was perceived to have made a misstep, I might be held in contempt of Court. I think that, in the Judge's mind, I am the bad guy – I don't think he holds anything against you. But I have to be careful, *and right*, or I could be in a world of trouble. We will need to update some of our discovery, and we need to be sure we don't offend the Judge at any stage before we go to trial."

"I'll keep that in mind, Ted. It's a shame we need to walk around on tip toes and can't just act like regular lawyers. But that's the hand we've been dealt, I guess. We have to play what we have," Jamie agreed, with resignation.

CHAPTER NINETEEN

A VISIT TO THE JUDGE

Ted found himself re-thinking and trying to find ways to deal with his bad relationship with Judge Newton. "The problem," he kept telling himself, "is that there is no way I can just meet with the Judge, sit down with him, and let him know I respect him and am sorry to have offended him, try to get on a better footing with him. But I cannot meet with him outside the presence of opposing counsel, and I obviously can't have the right kind of conversation with them present. It's in their interest for the bad relationship to stay bad. I could write a letter and send a copy to all counsel, but I am afraid it would look like I was trying to butter him up in advance of the trial, and it would lack the stamp of sincerity. A letter is just too cold and impersonal. If I do anything, it needs to be done in person, and that looks like an impossibility. Also, I have enough pride that I don't want to say I was wrong. I wasn't wrong. I'm sorry it happened the way it did, but I wasn't wrong. Guess I'll have to take it one day at a time and hope time does some healing."

Just then, Jamie Fletcher came into Ted's office with news. "Ted, I just got through talking with Judge Newton's law clerk about a discovery issue, and he told me Judge Newton was in the hospital for some sort of emergency surgery, don't know exactly what. Looks like he might be out for a few days, at least. What do you make of that?"

"I don't know what to think, Jamie. I certainly hope he is all right, or that he will be all right after his re-covery. Depending on what the medical problem is, our *AFCO* trial date cold be affected. Let me ponder it a bit," Ted said. Ted's almost immediate instinct was to go visit Judge Newton in the hospital, something he would likely have done as a matter of course, as he had made several hospital visits to other Judges and to other lawyers in the past. But the circumstances in this instance were unusu-al, due to his relationship problems with this Judge. If he went for the visit, it had to be a pure goodwill call, being careful to avoid any reference to the *AFCO* case, or their bad relations. Nor could he do anything to suggest he was trying to curry favour with the Judge. He checked with the hospital and found that Judge Newton was permitted to have visitors. Ted decided to make the visit.

Ted arrived at the hospital, inquired as to the room number, and took the elevator to the patient's floor, knocked on the door and heard a voice say, "Come on in." Ted entered the room and saw Judge Newton in bed, with his wife sitting in a chair beside the bed. "Well, if it isn't Ted Born!" said the Judge. "This is my wife, Nell."

"I'm glad to meet you, Mrs. Newton. I hope I haven't come at a bad time. I won't stay long, just wanted to wish you a good and speedy recovery," Born said.

"That's nice of you, Ted. I had a precancerous growth - they're checking to see if there's any real cancer there. I didn't want to waste any time getting it checked out, as it was in my cranium. I have a wonderful team of doctors, and they are taking good care of me. They are all so renowned, I felt like bowing to them. So, the surgery was three days ago, and is behind me, unless they find they didn't get it all. Hopefully, they are just going to observe me for a few more days and let me go," the Judge said.

"I'm sorry you had to go through this, but it looks like they're taking good care of you," Ted said.

"Well, I've been praying, too. I've got my Bible here, and I have been working on a Sunday School lesson – you know, I teach a Sunday School class at my Church. We all need prayers," Judge Newton said.

"No doubt about that. I know I need them, and I will add my prayers for a good report. Well, I have taken enough of your time. I do hope you get good news when you get back all the test results. I'll be going, but do take care. Really nice to meet you, Mrs. Newton. Goodbye," said Ted as he closed the door and left the hospital.

When Ted got back to his office, he called Jamie and asked if he could talk for a few minutes. Jamie came right over. "Jamie, I've just come back from the hospital where I had a brief visit with Judge Newton." Ted began.

"You *did!?* You *really did!!?* I don't believe it. How did it go?" asked Jamie.

"I really don't know, Jamie, except I have the impression it did no harm. The Judge was in bed, with his wife sitting by the bedside. Nothing was said about the case, nor about our relationship. He seemed cordial, but it was hard to tell whether it was a superficial cordiality in the presence of his wife, or perhaps because he was not expecting the visit and did not know what to think of it. He told me his surgery was in the cranium, a tumor his doctors think was noncancerous, but I have to wonder if this has been affecting his performance on the bench. I think it was a little awkward for both of us, but at least I did not detect any overt hostility or coolness relative to my visit.

"At least we have met as two human beings sharing good wishes and mentioning the virtue of prayer. You know, it was just two persons talking about health and blessings, not Judge and lawyer, although I was careful to show respect and good wishes. Of course, context is very important. We could have had a cordial visit in the context of a hospital room where his health was the focus, and then he could go back to his office, open up again the files on our *AFCO* case, and seethe with anger and indignation. In the context of our litigation, the past history may kick in and the bad relationship could come out again. I do think there was some benefit in 'de-horning' each of us to the other, the chance to see ourselves as caring individuals. And there was nothing superficial about it from my standpoint. I genuinely wish him all the best, and I know that he really is a good and conscientious Judge, at least when in good health. There is just something about this case, whatever it is, that has struck him the wrong way, and, in his mind, justice means we should lose. Somehow, we have to change that," Ted said.

"That's a big order, considering how adamantly and consistently he has rejected our view of the case. However, at least we now have TWO Court of Appeals decisions that tell him he should let the jury decide this case. That should count for something," Jamie said.

"They do count for something, and Judge Newton will dutifully let the case go to the jury this time. However, do not discount the power of the Judge to control what gets to the jury by his evidentiary rulings and his instructions to the jury. He can still powerfully influence the outcome, and we cannot kid ourselves into expecting a 180-degree change in his thinking, notwithstanding the Court of

Appeals. We still very much have a rough row to hoe."

"I am committed to working as hard as I can, Ted. In fact, I have some things I need to do right now," Jamie said.

"Just one more thing, Jamie. I think we probably should not mention this hospital visit to Anson Fowlkes, or to anyone else. Anson is so distressed and beside himself, I don't know how he might take it. Nor do I want the fact of the visit spread around, and, after all, the visit did not involve any discussion of Anson's case," Ted emphasized.

"Gotcha," Jamie reassured him.

CHAPTER TWENTY

DOONEY'S INFORMATION

Ted Born's telephone rang, and he saw it was Anson Fowlkes calling. Ted winced. Another phone call from Anson, wanting to know how the case is going, just like scores of telephone calls Ted had labored over in the past. He had nothing to tell Anson about the case that he had not already told him, discussing every option, every possibility, every strategy. It was one of the curses a lawyer must endure, with as much patience and composure as possible. It would be just another call among so many others, but at least a real trial would be coming up, and there was resolution foreseeable ahead.

Nevertheless, Ted took the call, and said, "Hello, Anson. Are you needing an update?" Ted asked.

"Well, an update is always welcome, but I really called to give you some new information that has just come to light. You know our salesman Dooney. He has stayed in touch off and on with one of my former employees who left with Clyde Enzor; they were always pretty good friends. His name is Fred Fitzpatrick. It seems Fred has had a falling out with Clyde and is no longer working with him – no longer employed by CECO. I'm not sure what the circumstances were that caused Fred to separate from CECO, but apparently it was acrimonious, and there's no love lost between Fred and Clyde. Dooney and Fred were having one of their conversations the other day, and Fred volunteered that there were a whole lot of things that went on at AFCO - things Clyde did - that Clyde has denied. And Fred said they were just wrong, but Clyde was the boss, and he needed financially to stay with Clyde at the time, so he kept his mouth shut. He says Clyde had the employees working late into the night copying all the business records of AFCO. He also said he was present while Clyde called customers and suppliers of AFCO, and Clyde wasn't a bit subtle about asking for a business relationship with them for his new company. Sounds very important to me," Anson said.

"Sounds important to me, too, Anson," said Ted. "Do you think this guy Fred has enough gumption to give us an affidavit to that effect, or – better yet – let us talk with him and prepare and print out an affidavit on the spot for him to sign?"

"I don't know, Ted. I didn't ask Dooney. I just got on the phone with you as soon as I got off the phone with Dooney. But I will call Dooney and see what he thinks. I have the impression that Fred is so resentful of Clyde that he just might do that. But Dooney is the one who needs to ask him. Let me check it out, and I'll call you back," Anson said.

Anson hung up and called Dooney. At the same time, Ted called Jamie Fletcher. "Jamie, can you come to my office? We just might have an important breakthrough in the *AFCO* case." Ted related his conversation with Anson. "Jamie, did we take the deposition of Fred Fitzpatrick? If we did, and if he lied on his deposition, then there would be credibility problems with his new revelations if he now gave an inconsistent deposition. On the other hand, if he's not on record supporting Clyde's story, we would be in good shape with his affidavit, but then I would have to wonder how we could have missed him in our earlier depositions."

"Ted, I don't recall that we ever took his deposition. We tried to be thorough, took Clyde's deposition and some of the employees, as well as some suppliers and customers, but it seems to me that there was one or two who were not available at the time. I think we were told Fred was in the hospital with some bad bone fractures from an accident. The others were so consistent with Clyde's script, we assumed it was pointless to take Fred's deposition, because he was going to have to say whatever Clyde told him to say. We probably should have gone ahead and taken the deposition later, when he was able to do it, but in retrospect he might not have come forward now if he would be contradicting his earlier sworn testimony. Maybe it was lucky that we didn't take his deposition earlier. Of course, we don't know whether he's going to have second thoughts, and clam up, deny he ever told Dooney what really happened," Jamie answered.

"Yeah, maybe we're in luck, though. I always thought we had a good circumstantial evidence case, but circumstantial evidence is never as good as direct evidence, and that's what's been lacking in our case up to now. You know, we have been wringing our hands, and Anson's been pulling his hair out, over the delays in this case, and I know how much Anson has been hurting on account of the delays. But the one good thing that might come out of the delays – if Fred will give us an affidavit – is that over time the conspiracy has unraveled. A lot of conspiracies do unravel, but it usually takes some time for that to happen. Now we have gotten this new and very helpful information just as we are getting ready to go back to trial. Manna from heaven!" Ted reflected, excitedly.

Just then, the phone rang, and it was Anson. "Ted, I've talked with Dooney, and Dooney says he thinks Fred is upset enough with Clyde that Fred just might put it on paper, give us an affidavit. He's going to call Fred and find out."

"Anson, if Fred is willing to give an affidavit, maybe he would be willing to come to our office to do it. It would be much more convenient to draft a proper affidavit, get all the details right, print it out and get it notarized in our office. Maybe Dooney could ask him, unless he feels it would 'spook' Fred to come to the offices of some strange lawyers. But we will find a way to get it done – somehow – if he just says he will sign an affidavit," Ted suggested. Anson said he would call Dooney back immediately, possibly reach him before he talks with Fred again, to test out whether Fred would sign and whether he would come to the lawyers' office.

Dooney got a positive response to the making of the affidavit *and* to coming to the office of Ted and Jamie to do it. Dooney accompanied Fred to the office, and Ted and Jamie greeted both men cordially. When they were seated in the conference room and coffee had been poured, Ted opened by saying, "Mr. Fitzpatrick, we all appreciate what you are doing. We know you are not here to do a favor for Anson or Dooney or for us by coming, or to hurt Clyde Enzor. You are here because it is the right thing to do. You are here because you know the difference between right and wrong and between justice and injustice. And it is people like you who make our system work, just by coming forward and telling the truth. That's all we ask you to do, and no one can ever say you were wrong to tell the truth, and you will never have any regrets for doing it. So, all we need today is just to put down on paper what you've told Dooney, and anything you would like to add. One other thing: By doing this, you will be freeing the other former AFCO employees so that they also will feel empowered to tell the truth."

Fred Fitzpatrick not only confirmed what he had previously told Dooney, but he said he still had in his possession a black looseleaf notebook containing information about certain AFCO customers, copied directly from AFCO files at Clyde's directions while still employed by AFCO, and taken with them secretly when they left. This would serve to verify the accuracy of Fred's recollection of the breaches of fiduciary duties that took place during the days before Clyde and his crew left AFCO to go into competition with their former company.

With the affidavit signed, Ted and Jamie filed with the Court a motion to require CECO and Arsenol to provide separate and independent counsel for all the former employees prior to the retaking of their depositions and during the ensuing trial. At the time the original depositions were taken, CECO and Arsenol had taken the position that their corporate counsel – David Slappey, et al. – could represent the employees as well as the trio of Clyde, CECO and Arsenol because, so they said, there was no conflict, as the employees' version of events was the same as Clyde's. The motion noted that now that one of the employees had credibly signed an affidavit challenging the unity of their respective stories, there would be a conflict of interest between Clyde with his version and that of the employees who were expected to have a different version. The new counsel for the employees needed to be in place soon so that the depositions of the former employees could be taken with advice of their new counsel not beholden to Clyde Enzor.

It was a bit surprising to Ted Born that Enzor, CECO and Arsenol did not argue the point, but in fact provided separate and independent counsel to the former AFCO employees at the expense of Arsenol and CECO. Ted wondered if the defendants might have received a phone call from the Judge's law clerk passing on the strong recommendation of Judge Newton that such independent counsel be provided. In any event, the depositions of the former employees were re-taken, and they essentially uniformly confessed agreement this time with Fred Fitzpatrick's version of events.

Ted wondered whether the bombshell affidavit of Fred, and the confirmatory depositions of the other former employees might cause the defendants to seek a settlement of the case, but that did not happen.

The pretrial conference was set, and Ted and Jamie prepared to go. They wondered what the Judge's attitude might be. He had seemed so hostile to Anson and AFCO throughout a lengthy litigation that it could not be predicted there would be any great change. Also, the defendants' lack of movement toward settlement could possibly mean that they were confident the Judge would still steer the result of a trial in a direction favorable to the defendants. Ted had had so many very uncomfortable moments in Judge Newton's Courtroom in recent months that he dreaded to have to go back into those Chambers for a pretrial conference. But this was a command event, no way to avoid it, so Ted went, with Jamie.

The lawyers assembled in Judge Newton's anteroom, waiting to enter the Judge's Chambers, an uncomfortable wait in Ted's case. At last, the Judge's Secretary ushered them in, and Ted looked warily to see if Lois Latimer was there, but she seemed to be absent. Upon entering the Chambers, Judge Newton came from behind his desk and headed directly for Ted Born and extended his hand. Ted took his hand, and Judge Newton held the handshake firmly, looking Ted in the eye and smiling. It was a moment forever embedded in Ted's memory. It was a sign that the exile was over, and perhaps the Promised Land was a bit nearer.   The resentment had vanished, replaced by acceptance and seeming admiration. Ted let his thoughts wander: "Could it be that he is congratulating me for believing in my client and in the client's case, and persevering through legal barricades and setbacks in order to achieve justice?" Ted knew in that instant that he was welcome and respected, restored to a sound and reconciled relationship that had been badly fractured.

Ted was almost embarrassed by the special reception he had received, and then the handshake was over, and Judge Newton moved on to the other lawyers and had a quick standard handshake with each of them. Everyone took a seat, and Judge Newton went over the pretrial Order item-by-item. Born asked that the Order include a prohibition of any mention at the trial of Anson's previous wives, or of the fact that he had, years ago, an alcohol problem. Judge Newton readily agreed to prohibit mention of Anson's prior wives, as that was irrelevant to any issues and very prejudicial to AFCO's case. As to the alcohol issue, the Judge was not inclined to exclude it altogether at this stage, because at one time it had affected Anson's relationship with at least some of the employees, even though it had been years earlier. However, he cautioned the defendants not to make an issue of it unless they were prepared to prove that it was a significant factor in the departure of Clyde and the other employees. He would make a final ruling on that point in the actual trial.

After finalizing all the other various elements of the pretrial Order, Judge Newton asked whether the parties had engaged in any settlement discussions. The attorneys responded that there had been none. Judge Newton then said, "I strongly urge you to get together and see if you can settle this case. This leopard has changed its spots. It's no longer the same case, and I can hear cash registers ringing in the distance." David Slappey volunteered that his clients did not believe they did anything wrong or illegal. They intended to contest the testimony of the employees, and they said that in any event, any copying that occurred was for convenience only and not actually necessary, as they had all the information in their heads anyway. Also, Enzor was going to deny the reported conversations between himself and suppliers and customers while still employed as an AFCO Vice President. The Judge just looked straight at the defense lawyers and said, "I think you would be wise to settle this case. That is all I intend to say. It is of course up to you. But this case needs to be settled. That's all. We are adjourned."

Ted and Jamie went back to their office for a "post-mortem" on the hearing. "What a relief, Ted, to go into a hearing or conference in Judge Newton's Court and not get all tensed up by his attitude toward us! He seemed to be telling us all - for a change - that he thought we had a good case, and that was a new experience for us. However, the defendants didn't seem worried, and that makes *me* feel worried," Jamie said in a happy celebratory mood.

Ted replied, "I feel the same way, Jamie, only more so, I'm sure, because Judge Newton's wrath was directed specifically at me. What I can't understand is the defendants' apparent desire to go on and try this case. Not only do we have this new evidence, which is damning to them, but Clyde has been lying under oath, and he's been exposed. What kind of credibility can he hope to have with the jury? I know the defense lawyers have been telling their clients now for the duration of this case that they were going to win, and they have had celebrations with Champagne to gloat over their past 'wins' on the directed verdict and then on summary judgment, and it must be embarrassing to turn around at this late date and tell them their case is a loser. Still, it doesn't make sense to ignore the present realities of the case. The only thing I can figure is that they hope Anson and AFCO will collapse financially sometime before the actual trial, which is still a month off, or that Anson is or will be hurting so badly that he will beg the defendants to settle at a bargain basement price. And, of course, even if we win the case, it can be appealed, and Arsenol will have no difficulty putting up a bond to delay having to pay anything until the appeal is decided, which could take up to two years, conceivably. Maybe their game is attrition, feeling they can still win because of the advantage of their heavily mismatched resources, even if they lose in Court. Of course, if they lose on appeal, they will have to pay interest on the judgment, and that will cost them, but they have the deep pockets of Arsenol to cover the interest, so I'm sure they aren't terribly worried. Anyway, that is for the future. Our job now is to get this case ready for trial, once again!"

CHAPTER TWENTY-ONE

TRIAL AT LAST

Ted and Jamie prepared for trial, settling on the order in which they would call witnesses, preparing
the witnesses by reviewing with them their expected testimony, being sure all exhibits were pre-marked and ready
to go, and working on jury selection and the opening
statement. They thought there might be a bare possibility
that the defendants would initiate settlement discussions,
despite their apparent disinterest displayed at the pretrial
conference. But there was only silence. Ted, Jamie and
their paralegal continued their preparation.

On the Thursday before the Trial was to have started
on the following Monday, the mail brought good news.
The Georgia Supreme Court rendered its advisory opinion, requested by the Eleventh Circuit, interpreting the

Georgia law on corporate dissolutions, opining that, once the time had expired for a dissolved corporation to be reinstated, it could neither sue nor be sued, for any reason, in any context. "This should sew up the appeal in the Eleventh Circuit," Ted said to Jamie. "But I wonder if Pure Fision will send us another round of flowers and Champagne," Ted joked.

"Not yet, in any event," Jamie said with a grin. "We haven't entirely won until the Eleventh Circuit speaks. But I hope that will be soon. Meanwhile, the *AFCO* case beckons."

The Monday morning of trial inevitably came, and Ted and Jamie found themselves in a Courtroom with a lot of potential jurors. The Judge had not approved a request Ted made for a jury questionnaire to be submitted for each juror to fill out, so there was initially little information about the jury pool other than the sea of faces staring at them, and a list of names and addresses. Moreover, the Judge, after asking the qualifying questions to verify basic eligibility for jury service, began asking them questions which might be specifically relevant to any bias that might affect their consideration of the case. Ted was especially interested in whether the jurors were employed, and, if so, where, as well as marital status, previous litigation involvement. whether they or any family members had involvement in other civil or criminal litigation After the Judge asked his questions of the jury, he asked if the lawyers for the parties had any further questions. Ted, conscious that Judge had left open the possibility that Anson's past alcohol history might be allowed in the case, asked the Judge to inquire further whether the jurors or any family members had experienced any alcohol addiction or drug addiction problems. Ted and Jamie were furiously making notes as to which jurors had made responses to the Judge's various questions, and the substance of the responses. This being a Federal Court civil jury, there would be only six jurors plus two alternates selected to hear the case, the alternates to be excused at the end of the evidence unless they were needed to replace one of the regular jurors who for some reason would be unable to complete his or her jury service.

The lawyers began striking the jurors, and Ted was glad to see that one of the jurors who had not been struck had operated a small business and could likely relate to Anson Fowlke's status as a business owner. There were four women and two men comprising the first six, and two of the six were African Americans, very much like the jury that heard the plaintiff's part of the first, aborted trial. Overall, the jury seemed to be a group that, at least, did not have obvious biases against AFCO or its case.

After a short break the jurors that had been selected took their seats in the jury box, and it was time for opening statements, following a few comments by the Judge. Representing the plaintiffs, Ted was entitled to go first with his statement. "Ladies and gentlemen, we very much appreciate your service on this jury. I know that each of you probably has other things you would rather be doing, but you are here performing a crucially important role in our system of justice. We cannot ask for more or less than fairness and justice. We expect the evidence to show that our client, Mr. Anson Fowlkes, started a business called AFCO some twenty years ago. It was all his idea, the business filled a need its customers had, and it turned out to be a good business that grew through the years and provided a living for Mr. Anson and his employees and their families. Among his employees was Mr. Clyde Enzor. Mr. Fowlkes brought him into his company, taught him the business, introduced him to customers and suppliers, and rewarded him with pay increases and promotions, eventually naming him Vice President of the company and trusting him to act in the best interests of the company. In fact, he turned over to Mr. Enzor more and more of the responsibility for running the company, with Mr. Fowlkes stepping back as he got older.

"However, there came a time when Mr. Enzor decided he wanted to take this company away from Mr. Fowlkes and make it his own. So, he devised a scheme where he would secretly prepare another office and warehouse space to be occupied by his new business when he would commence competition with Mr. Fowlke's company. He made deals with almost all of AFCO's employees to take them with him, as well as getting most of the customers and suppliers to switch over to him. As his plot gained steam, he made a deal with Arsenol - one of AFCO's major suppliers and another defendant in this case - to deliver the business to Arsenol for a very handsome up-front profit for himself, plus, he would get a very generous compensation package to manage the new business. Also, before resigning from AFCO, he and the employees who were leaving to go into competition with AFCO began copying the records of AFCO to take with them, so they would have all the inside information from their former employer. They even planned it so not all the employees would quit at once. They planned to leave some of them behind for a while who could keep Enzor current with all that Mr. Fowlkes was doing. And then they also would leave, pursuant to a pre-planned agreement to join the others who would have already left. He carried all of this out in secret, behind Mr. Fowlkes' back. And when he was ready, he turned in his resignation to Mr. Fowlkes, and told Mr. Fowlkes falsely that he was going on a cruise, which he did not do and never intended to do.

"Now, Mr. Fowlkes understands that he must expect fair competition, which in our economy is a fact of life and is generally a good thing. But there was nothing fair about this. They secretly concocted this plot and worked to carry it out while they were still on AFCO's payroll, and while Clyde Enzor was an officer – a Vice President and essentially chief operating officer of AFCO. He was getting paid by AFCO to be loyal and to work for the best interests of AFCO, and all the while he was doing every-thing he could do to destroy AFCO. This was plainly and simply UNFAIR competition and a breach of his duty of loyalty to the company that was paying him. We call it a breach of a fiduciary duty, this duty of loyalty owed by an officer of a company to the one who was paying him to be loyal. And Arsenol was an accomplice in all this, working with Enzor to undermine its own customer and to reap the benefit of Enzor's disloyalty. In fact, it is questionable whether Enzor could have pulled off his scheme without the support of Arsenol, which got itself a new subsidiary corporation at what we will show was a bargain price.

"One other thing. You may or may not agree whether Anson Fowlkes would be a good candidate for sainthood. None of us is perfect. But that is not the issue before us. The issue is whether he was wronged, and whether the defendants are liable to him because they committed wrongs toward him for which he is entitled to just compensation as the law provides. We will address the damages issue in this trial, as well as all the wrongs that entitle AFCO to compensation, because this once prosperous company has now been devastated - destroyed - by the wrongdoing of the defendants, just as they had planned and plotted. I ask you, and know you will, give thoughtful attention to the evidence as we present it. Thank you for your service."

The Judge then nodded to David Slappey to make an opening statement on behalf of the defendants. "Ladies and Gentlemen, you have just heard a version of the facts in this case from the plaintiffs, and it was a partisan statement which we as defendants see very differently. First, bear in mind that Anson Fowlkes could have insisted that his employees enter into non-compete agreements, which he did not do. Maybe he should have, but he did not. He also could have insisted that his employees all enter into confidentiality agreements, as well, designating company records and information that were confidential and that could not be disclosed or used competitively against the company AFCO. Maybe he should have, but he didn't. All the employees at AFCO, including Clyde Enzor, were what we call 'employees at will.' There were no employment agreements of any kind. Anson Fowlkes could have fired any of them at any time, and they would have been out on the street, with no recourse. By the same token, the employees, including Clyde Enzor, were free to leave at any time, and they were not under any obligation to give Anson Fowlkes any notice or any reason relative to their leaving the company.

"It also is completely permissible for employees at will, as Clyde and the others were, to make plans for what they will be doing after they leave, including going into competition with AFCO, as long as they were doing their jobs at AFCO that they were being paid to do. We do not believe there will be any evidence that Clyde or any of the other employees slacked off or didn't fully and competently perform their job and duties while they were working there. Clyde will testify that he never told any employees to copy records of AFCO to take with them, and if any of them did that, they did it on their own, and, in any case, there wasn't anything confidential about those documents. None of them were marked confidential, and all the information in them was well known to the employees anyway, as they worked closely with suppliers and customers and had all that information in their heads. They were certainly entitled to take with them, when leaving AFCO, all the information in their heads, and so it is immaterial whether they also had copies of some papers with the same information on them.

"In our nation and economy, we put a high value on two things: First, we believe that every person has the right to make choices about how to better oneself, to change jobs for a better job, to help their families have a better future. The second thing is that we believe in competition. Competition brings prices down, prevents gouging and outrageous profits, and is good for the consumer. That is the way we look at what happened in this case, and we do not think you as jurors will want to roll back the clock to lock these employees into a job from which there is no escape, and thereby reduce competition, all of which would just hurt consumers. Just bear in mind that this case must be judged on the basis of the evidence you will hear, not on the words you have heard from the plaintiff's lawyer. I think that is all that needs to be said at this time. The evidence will speak for itself. Thank you."

Judge Newton then looked toward the plaintiffs' table and said, "The plaintiffs may call their first witness." Ted Born said he would call Clyde Enzor as an adverse and hostile witness. The defendants' lawyers seemed surprised, as they likely expected the plaintiffs' case would start off with Anson Fowlkes as a witness, exactly what Born was hoping, that Enzor would not be well prepared to be the lead-off witness. After some introductory preliminary questions, Born got into the substance of the case.

Born: "Mr. Enzor, you were an officer of AFCO for some years, were you not, in fact you had the office of Vice President, the second highest office in the company, did you not?"

Enzor: "I was, and I worked hard."

Born: "And you knew you served in a position of trust and owed AFCO the duty of complete and undivided loyalty?"

Enzor: "I was always loyal while I worked there."

Born: "But you knew you were obligated to be totally loyal and trustworthy because of your position as an officer and chief operating officer of AFCO, did you not?"

Enzor: "I knew that, and I was."

Born: "When did you tell the other employees you would be leaving AFCO?"

Enzor: "I don't remember exactly."

Born: "We have testimony from several of the other employees that they worked for about six weeks with you to get a new location ready for your planned new business. Would that be correct?"

Enzor: "It could be. So, maybe I told them about six weeks before I left."

Born: "Why did you tell them, Mr. Enzor?"

Enzor: "Well, they had been working with me a long time, and I thought I owed it to them."

Born: "But you didn't tell it to Dooney McNab, who was also an employee. Why not?"

Enzor: "I just missed getting to him somehow. I didn't feel close to him."

Born: "But you had worked with him for years, more than with most of the others. You didn't feel you owed him the same 'courtesy' you showed the others?"

Enzor: "I couldn't depend on him. He might have told Anson."

Born: "Why would that have been a problem? And why didn't you tell Anson Fowlkes yourself?"

Enzor: "Anson would have fired me, if I had told him, and I wasn't ready yet to be fired. It would have been premature. It would have ruined everything."

Born: "Did you pledge the other employees to secrecy?"

Enzor: "Of course. After they all begged me to let

them come with me. We couldn't afford to let Anson know ahead of time that we were leaving."

Born: "How did you know the employees would all agree to come with you? If they had decided not to go with you, what would have kept them from telling Anson?"

Enzor: "Nothing. But I knew my men, and I knew they would keep it quiet."

Born: "Did you think they would keep it quiet because you promised them pay raises if they came with you? I want to advise you, before you answer, that we have a lot of deposition testimony from the employees that you actually invited them to come and offered them bonuses and pay raises if they did."

Enzor: "I did tell them they could expect bonuses and pay raises, but only after they told me they wanted to come with me."

Born: "You understand, Mr. Enzor, that the employees don't remember it that way. Do you want to reconsider your answer?"

Enzor: "I knew in my heart I was doing the right thing for myself and for them."

Born: "Did you know in your heart that you were doing the right thing for AFCO and Anson Fowlkes by keeping it a secret from them that you and almost all your salespeople would be walking out?"

Enzor: "I don't know. It would not have worked if I had told Anson."

Born: "But you had known Mr. Fowlkes longer than you had known any of the others, and he had given you pay raises and bonuses and promotions through all those years. You didn't feel you owed him at least the same courtesy you felt you owed the employees, to tell him you would be leaving?"

Enzor: "I felt like I was doing my job. I didn't have to tell him."

Born: "Was it a part of your job to take AFCO's employees away with you?"

Enzor: "I knew in my heart it was all right to leave and set up my own business with employees I had come to know."

Born: "Is it your idea that you were being a loyal officer of AFCO while you were trying secretly to get its employees to leave AFCO and come with your new company? Is that your idea of loyalty?"

Enzor: "I had a right to do that."

Born: "Did you understand that you were more than an employee of AFCO - you were an officer, Vice President of the company - and that, as an officer, you owed an especially high duty of loyalty to AFCO?"

Enzor: "I don't know how to answer that. I just felt in

my heart it was all right, what I was doing."

Born: "We have testimony that some of the other employees heard you on the telephone urging suppliers and customers to work with you. Did you feel in your heart that taking away from AFCO its lifeline of suppliers and customers, was all right, while you were being paid as an officer of AFCO to work solely for its benefit and to do it no harm?"

Enzor: "I didn't tell them not to do business with AFCO. I just wanted them to do business with me."

Born: "Couldn't you have waited until you left AFCO to contact the customers and suppliers of AFCO, and not do it while you were supposed to be working for the best interests of AFCO?"

Enzor: "It might not have worked if I had waited. I had to line them up ahead of time. What's wrong with a little competition? I knew in my heart I was doing the right thing, just trying to get off on the right foot with my customers and suppliers."

Born: "And then you told your employees who were going with you to copy the key records of AFCO so they could take them along to the new business. Did you feel in your heart it was right to take records that did not belong to you, but belonged to AFCO? In your book, Mr. Enzor, wouldn't that be like stealing something that did not belong to you?"

Enzor: "Well, I looked at it like this. First, we all worked hard to produce the data, make the sales and all that, so I felt we had an interest in the data. Second, we had most of it in our head anyway, so what was the harm of taking it with us on paper?"

Born: "You remember, Mr. Enzor, testifying under oath at an earlier stage of this lawsuit, that no such copying of AFCO's business records had occurred. Why did you not tell the truth then?"

Enzor: "I just didn't remember it before. Then, I was reminded when some of the employees gave their testimony a little while back."

Born: "If it's true that all of you had the data in your heads, why would you have bothered to copy it? Actually, you needed the paper records, didn't you?"

Enzor: "All I can say is, it was more convenient to have it on paper, but wasn't necessary."

Born: "But you knew it was AFCO's data, not yours, and you and the employees were paid good money to get those data on the books for AFCO, not for you?"

Enzor: "That's a technicality. I knew in my heart I was doing the right thing."

Born: "And when you finally sprang on Mr. Fowlkes that you were leaving, you told him you were 'going on a cruise,' didn't you? Why didn't you tell him the truth, Mr. Enzor?"

Enzor: "I didn't think it was any of his business what I was planning to do."

Born: "Only that you were going to take away his employees, his customers and suppliers – and that wasn't any of his business? Why could you not have at least been honest with Anson Fowlkes after you had resigned?"

Enzor: "I just wanted to leave, didn't want to get into any long discussions with him."

Born: "And you never told him that on the very next morning several of AFCO's other employees would be re-signing, with a few hanging back as 'fifth column' spies?"

Enzor: "We didn't talk about who else would be leaving. None of us had employment contracts or non-compete agreements."

The testimony of Clyde Enzor continued as he went into the circumstances that led to Arsenol buying out Enzor's new company. He said he had his heart set on going into business on his own, but then realized it was going to take more money than he had anticipated, and he worked out a deal with Arsenol to buy the new business at a premium and to ensure a pay raise for himself and the employees going forward. For Arsenol, it was a bargain, because it could never have set up such a business with experienced salespersons and fairly certain profits if it had been necessary to start from scratch. Arsenol had been in on the plans for a good month or more before Clyde Enzor's resignation, and participated in the secrecy, which Born believed made Arsenol a co-conspirator, equally guilty with Enzor and CECO, and really an indispensable co-conspirator without which Enzor's scheme would not have worked.

David Slappey, on cross-examination of his own witness asked some softball questions, not willing to risk what Enzor might say if asked unrehearsed questions. He asked if there were any employment agreements, non-compete agreements, or confidentiality agreements, and whether any of the documents copied bore any kind of "Confidential" stamp on them. He asked Enzor if he knew whether any of the AFCO suppliers or customers had continued to do business with AFCO, to which Enzor testified he knew of at least some business, but he acknowledged CECO seemed to be getting most of the business. At a sidebar conference at the end of Slappey's questioning, Judge Newton instructed Slappey to ask all the questions of Enzor that he intended to ask, because he would not permit Slappey to put Enzor back on the witness stand during the defendants' part of the case. Slappey thought about that for a moment, conferred with his co-counsel and decided he would terminate his examination and would waive the opportunity to call Enzor back to the witness stand for any further questions during the defense part of the case. Born had no further questions on re-direct, and Judge Newton recessed the proceedings for the day, to resume the next morning.

Back at their office, Born and Fletcher reflected on the first day of trial. "Ted, I think your questioning of Clyde Enzor went very, very well, and Slappey did nothing to rehabilitate him. I feel like the defense never saw it coming, never expected you to call Enzor as an adverse and hostile witness, right out of the box – bang!" Jamie offered.

Born responded, "I thought so also, but it's good to have the viewpoint of someone not directly engaged in the heat of the examination battle, as you can be more objective. My eye contact with the jury told me they were getting our point, but you can never be sure. Here's what I am inclined to do. I want to call one of the employees – I think Fred Fitzpatrick. Then we can just read into evidence the depositions of the other employees; I don't think we need to put them on the stand 'live' because Clyde now basically concedes the accuracy of their testimony. Then we need testimony of Arsenol's business development manager, which we could do 'live' or via deposition. Again, Clyde doesn't really deny the facts and Arsenol really doesn't contest them, except maybe on some immaterial details. Better put the manager on notice to appear, and we can decide later whether to put his testimony in 'live' or by deposition. We don't want to subject the jury to a lot of repetitious and uncontested testimony, but Arsenol is a major defendant, and it might be better for us to call their man as an adverse witness, like Clyde, rather than have the defendants put him on after rehearsing him. Then we will go with Anson. We have to be careful with him. You know the old saying among litigators: 'it is more blessed to cross-examine than to examine.' If your own witness does not come across well, it can be devastating. On the other hand, if you don't do so well on cross-examination, the jury will cut you some slack, because they don't expect you to make a lot of points with a guy on the other side of the case (although I think we did, with Clyde). But if you don't do well with your own witness, the jury will really take notice and it will be a major point in the later jury deliberations. Anson has a great story to tell but sometimes he gets wordy. He has to be credible and natural, and I don't want to cramp his style too much, but he can be loquacious. He wants to tell his life's story and will wander all over the place if we let him. I've advised - warned - him to rein in his instincts, but I will keep my fingers crossed until he gets off the stand. Finally, there is our economist who will be black-boarding damages, more than three million dollars. I think that will wrap up our case. Jamie, you handle Fred Fitzpatrick and the other employee depositions. I will take Anson – I think he expects me to do his questioning – and you take the economist. Then we will see what the defense does. They can't call Clyde, because they have elected not to do so. I don't think they will call any of the employees. They could call someone from Arsenol, but we will have already called the guy who would be the princi-pal witness from Arsenol. They will put on their expert witness contesting our damages, but I can't figure who else they could call. There's no one else on their witness list. It looks like they're just going to argue that Anson has nobody to blame but himself because he didn't have an employment agreement, or non-compete agreement or confidentiality agreement with any of the employees. So, they could leave at any time, without consequences, providing competition for Anson and AFCO, which is a good thing for consumers. But that just isn't the law. You can have unfair competition without reference to the various types of agreements he focuses on. Sure, they could always leave and go into competition with AFCO, but only if it is a clean leave."

"Ted, do you think the defense lawyers really believe their version of the law will be bought by the Judge and jury? Surely, they know better. Think they might try to settle with us even at this late date?" Jamie probed.

Ted shook his head. "It would be logical, but I don't think so. If they were inclined to settle, they would have initiated a move before trial got started. They either think we will stumble badly somewhere, maybe in Anson's testimony, or that we will alienate the jury, or that Judge Newton's original hostility to our position will come to the fore again and bail them out. I think they have so much pride tied up in this case, and the lawyers have told their clients so many times that their case is a winner, they can't bring themselves to backtrack. But Judge Newton so far seems to hold firm to his position that 'this leopard has changed its spots.' We know what we need to do. Let's do it."

CHAPTER TWENTY-TWO

RESOLUTION

Ted and Jamie had done what they could. The jury had heard the evidence and the closing arguments, and now the Judge was giving instructions to the jury. A key concern was whether the Judge would give one important instruction requested by the Born/Fletcher team: "If you find that the plaintiffs engaged in unfair competition or a breach of a fiduciary duty, this would establish liability whether or not there were employment agreements, non-compete agreements, or confidentiality agreements between AFCO and any of the employees." That proposed instruction would be a correct statement of the law, but Ted's concern was that the Judge might hold back because it would sound a lot like a directed verdict for plaintiffs, a mandate that the jury bring in a verdict for the plaintiffs, a step further than Judge Newton might wish to go, especially given his previous hostility to the plaintiffs' case. The Judge had told the lawyers what to expect on all other instructions, but he had reserved judgment on this one. Now the parties would find out what the Judge had decided. Judge Newton hesitated for a moment, and then he gave the requested instruction. David Slappey looked crestfallen; Ted and Jamie looked very pleased. In a sidebar conference, the defendants noted their objection to the instruction and suggested modifications, but the Judge overruled the exception and declined to amend his challenged instruction.

The jury was sent to the jury room to begin its deliberations. Ted and Jamie shook hands, then moved into a cloakroom where they could talk privately while awaiting the jury's verdict, accompanied by Anson Fowlkes who had sat at the table with them as the company representative for AFCO. Anson spoke first: "Ted and Jamie, however this comes out, I will forever be grateful to you for sticking with me through some rough times, times when I almost lost my mind, suffering in a way I can never express to you, times when I doubted there was any justice in the world. We had so many setbacks – not your fault, but still almost terminal setbacks – I can't allow myself to be optimistic. But you've given me hope, and I can't imagine how the trial could have gone any better, regardless how the jury comes out. I just have to live the rest of my life knowing we gave it the best shot we could give, with the best team of lawyers I can imagine."

"Thank you, Anson. We've walked down that lonely road, too, and there were times we had our doubts as to whether we would ever win this case, ever get justice for you, and it all hinges now on those six people in the jury room. At least this time we felt we had a level playing field. The Judge was fair, despite all that happened in the past. We just needed to be able to put your case before the six, and now we wait and see. Of course, this is about more than winning. Even if we win, it's a question about how much money the jury awards you. We haven't really won unless you get made whole. So, everything is on the line. I thought you did fine, Anson, when you were on the witness stand. You answered the questions, didn't wander around. There was a sadness and reflectiveness about you that was appropriate for someone who has gone through all you have suffered. The defendants never tried to bring up the negatives from the past. Of course, the Judge had admonished them not to do it, but it would not have surprised me if they had not tried to find a way to argue you had 'opened up' the subjects of alcohol and your marriages. I would like to think it was decency on their part that they did not try to bring it up, but I also think they might have been just smart enough to know that kind of thing might boomerang against them, badgering you over ancient irrelevancies in an effort to compensate for their wrongdoing. Anyway, here we wait. Want to go downstairs and get a mid-afternoon snack?"

The parties waited and waited. Nobody on either side broached the subject of a possible settlement. It was too late for that now, given all that had transpired in the case. But then the word came, "the jury has a verdict." The Judge told the Marshall to bring the jurors back to the Courtroom to deliver the verdict. The Judge opened the verdict form, read it silently and then announced, "The jury form has checked the boxes that say they have found in favor of plaintiff AFCO and against the defendants Clyde Enzor, CECO and Arsenol. They have assessed compensatory damages in the amount of Two Million Dollars and punitive damages in the amount of One Million Dollars. Do you wish to poll the jury?" The polling was done, and the jurors stuck by their verdict, as they usually do. The Judge then thanked the jury and discharged them. There was a three-way hug among Ted, Jamie and Anson, and they hung on to each other for what seemed a full minute. Judge Newton smiled and retired to his Chambers. Lois Latimer was nowhere around.

Ted and Jamie gathered their files and went back to the office, arriving just in time to hear an announcement over the intercom: "Ted Born and Jamie Fletcher have just won a jury verdict for a total of Three Million Dollars. Please congratulate them."

Lawyers, paralegals and secretaries descended on Ted's office with congratulations. Ted said, "This is not the biggest verdict we've ever won, but it was one of the hardest. And most memorable. It took two trips to the Court of Appeals before we ever got the opportunity for a full trial, and in the process, we got on the wrong side of a Federal Judge, although I hasten to say our good relationship with that Judge has now been fully restored. The client at one point was unable to pay us to continue our work, so we made a partial contingency deal, which will well compensate us but will still leave the client - a small company - with enough money to be made whole. There may be an appeal, and I expect there will be, but I don't have much doubt we will ultimately prevail. One good thing is that the judgment can definitely be collected, because one of the defendants is a big company with enormous net worth, and there's almost certainly insurance as well. Jamie did a great job, as he always does. I don't think I could have made it without his energy, resourcefulness, and good judgment – plus gobs of talent. You would think he had been practicing law for decades. He deserves an awful lot of the credit."

When the crowds thinned out, Jamie said, "Ted, thank you for letting me tag along with you. This has been an incredible journey and experience. I want to talk with you some more tomorrow. Right now, I need to get back home to a wife and young daughter I am afraid have not seen much of me lately."

"Sure, Jamie, there's not a whole lot else to talk about anyway, and I feel fairly drained myself, now that some of the euphoria has worn off. I think I will head for home also, and to a wife who has suffered through this ordeal as much as I have," Ted declared.

Jamie left, and Ted's secretary came in and pointed to a stack of mail. "Before you leave, here's the mail that has accumulated since you have been in trial. I haven't opened any of it, but I noticed that there is an envelope from the Eleventh Circuit where you have that *Pure Fision* appeal pending. I know you want to get out of here and get some rest, but I thought you just might want to open that one first."

Ted opened the envelope. It was an Order of the Eleventh Circuit affirming the dismissal of the pending appeal, based on the absence of a qualified plaintiff, as the proffered plaintiff had been dissolved and was ineligible for reinstatement, not competent to sue of be sued, citing the advisory opinion of the Supreme Court of Georgia. "WOW!" said Ted, and "Hallelujah! Looks like I've seen the last of that case that just wouldn't go away. I'll call the client and suggest they send another installment of flowers and Champagne! Jamie deserves a lot of the credit, too, since he is the one who first discovered that the plaintiff Gas Up had been dissolved. I'll make sure he sees this affirmance first thing tomorrow, in case he didn't get a copy in the mail."

The next day, Ted and Jamie got together again, did the usual post-mortem on the *AFCO* case, but a joyous post-mortem in this instance, as well as celebrating the win in the *Pure Fision* civil case. "Our bottler client will never know how fortunate it was to get out of that class action treble damage case at this early stage. Most of those cases go on forever, and the defendant company ends up paying big bucks because it's cheaper than paying lawyers to continue with the litigation, and, of course, if they lose, it's practically the end of the world for many of them, being liable for treble damages, plus the plaintiff's legal fees, plus their own legal fees. To the client at this stage, they think our win in the *Pure Fision* civil case is just getting rid of a minor annoyance. They'll never know. But that's life, I guess," Ted said.

Jamie nodded, was quiet for a moment, then looked up at Ted and said, "Ted, I've got to tell you something. It's been on my mind for several weeks now, but I didn't want to mention it while we were getting ready for trial and then going to trial in the *AFCO* case. You know, I think of myself as still being fairly young, although I have matured a whole lot working with you on these cases. It's been invaluable to me as a lawyer, but also to me as a person. Never could I have imagined I could ever have learned so much in such a short few years. I've also worked with a lot of other lawyers here in the Firm, too, and they are all fine lawyers, but what I've learned from you is special. I've learned about how to handle cases, deal with clients – deal with Judges, above all – but what I have learned from you about integrity and judgment and competence has changed me. I'm different now."

"Jamie, I appreciate your saying all those nice things, and I can tell you are entirely sincere, and that's why I will always remember this conversation we've had. I don't know it all, Jamie. I'm still learning too, and I look forward for us as a team to get better and better. As you know, I also have worked, and still work, with a lot of other lawyers here in the Firm, but things seem to click especially well when you and I team up, not to take anything away from the others I work with," Ted responded.

"That's just it, Ted. It would be such a special thing to continue working with you, but, you see, I not only have a wife, but now I have a daughter, and she's the apple of my eye, and I'm not seeing much of her, and I feel guilty, and like I'm missing something that I virtually live for. And we're hoping for our family to grow, and my wife is after me to get more regular hours and more family hours. So, I have gotten an offer I can't turn down. I didn't go out looking for it, but, somehow, they got my name and they checked me out and they want me to come be their inhouse counsel, at least on litigation matters, and the money is good – although this is not about money – and the hours are good, usually nine to five every day, with occasional out-of-town trips. You better believe I'll be remembering you, and I hope I can make some referrals to you. I'll be leaving in two weeks. I accepted the job two weeks ago, but I didn't want to tell you and disrupt the trial preparations then. One other thing: I'll have to move to Charleston, so it will be quite a change for me. We'll be living in an apartment or something until we can find the house we want, and we'll also have to sell our present house. I'll miss working with you, Ted," Jamie offered.

The blood appeared to drain from Ted's face. "I'm speechless, Jamie. I've come to think of you as family, and you are family, in a sense. All of us here at the Firm spend so much time with each other, and we like each other and work well together – we think of ourselves here as a big family, and to lose you is to lose a member of my family. We have a lot of great lawyers, but lawyers aren't fungible. They all bring their unique personalities and talents, and relationships mean so much. I wish you'd say 'it ain't so,' that this is just a bad dream and that I will wake up and find it really didn't happen. But that's selfish of me. My interest, and the interest of the Firm, is always to be supportive of whatever is best personally for the lawyers who do us the honor of coming and working with us. So, I reluctantly have to say good luck and God be with you and your family. If you ever have a change of mind, and I don't expect you will, just remember where we are. To us, you will always be a part of our extended family. As is true for every family, what is best for you is what we want for you. Still, that won't keep us from missing you."

Jamie rose from the chair across the desk from Ted, extended his hand, which Ted grasped firmly, and then he turned, opened the office door, and closed it. Ted sat for a moment. Then the door opened again, and Jamie stuck his head in again. "Ted, I'm still interested in that case you have with the photo of the naked wife on the computer. That's one I'm sorry I missed out on."

"I'll update you as we go along, Jamie, by email at your new job, if necessary. It will give me an excuse to stay in touch. Right now, the case is looking very good. The bad guys have fired their lawyers and have replaced them with some others who should be a little more reasonable to work with. They've been hinting they want to settle the case, and in this instance, that means, how much are *they* willing to pay *us*! We will want a real good settlement to compensate our guys for what they've gone through, almost losing their livelihoods, having to fend off the FBI and threatened criminal prosecutions, as well as emotional trauma. It's possible it could come to an end fairly soon. We'll have to see, but our guys are expecting several million dollars, and I think they ought to get it."

"Thanks, Ted. Let me hear from you on the final chapter of that one. In the meantime, I'll be missing you and all my friends here in the Firm. You are right. I have come to think of all of you as family. This move is going to take some adjusting. I just feel I've gotta do it. Bye," and Jamie closed the door again.

Ted turned his desk chair so he could see out the glass wall behind him. But it was all a blur. He looked without seeing. It was all motion down on the street, but the big picture never seemed to change. "I know what I ought to be telling myself. I should be saying, 'Ted, you will some and you lose some. You've been winning cases, and you should be glad for that. Life has to go on, just as it went on before Jamie ever came to the Firm. Change is the law of life.' It's all true, but this particular change is so sudden, such a shock. I just wasn't prepared. We worked together so well. Maybe it's time for me to learn what Jamie has already learned, that I need to spend more time with my own family at home, and less with my family at the Firm. I'm sure I've shortchanged them to serve the jealous mistress that is the LAW, and I do have such a great wife and family at home! The law office is not the living end."

He flipped through some more of his mail from the previous day. There was a note to call Universal Tire. Apparently, Universal's house counsel has a new case he wanted to discuss. It seems to be an exploding tire case over in Phoenix County. A Universal tire had blown out and the car had gone off the road and hit a Mock Orange tree. Bad injuries and a death. "I guess I'll call and talk with them about it first thing tomorrow. I'm grateful I get contacted to handle new cases, but I would prefer to get some cases that are winnable. This one seems impossible. I might have to postpone my vow to spend more time with the family. It's the fate of a lawyer."

ABOUT THE AUTHOR

Thad Long is an author and versatile attorney, with decades of practice handling difficult trials and other matters for defendants and plaintiffs in a changing litigious environment. This most recent release, "The Jury Has a Verdict!" is the third of a trilogy of "Ted Born" Courtroom drama books and is a prequel to "The Impossible Mock Orange Trial," with "The Vow: Ted Born's Last Trial" being set as the sequel to the other two. The author's books have received rave Amazon reviews for accurately depicting journeys through the anatomy of high-stakes trials, with climactic endings. "The Jury Has a Verdict!" takes the reader on a you-are-there tour of the challenges, triumphs and anguish of Ted Born's difficult interactions with Judges and juries, as he seeks justice for his clients while maintaining deference to the judiciary. Mr. Long took his undergraduate degree from Columbia University with a major in physics and his law degree from the University of Virginia where he served as Comments & Projects Editor of the *Virginia Law Review* and was tapped for Order of the Coif, the Raven Society and Omicron Delta Kappa. He has consistently been listed in *Best Lawyers in America* for more than thirty years, recognizing him for his abilities in an extraordinary nine different areas of expertise. He is also an elected life member of the prestigious American Law Institute. He has recently been honored with the Lifetime Achievement Award from Marquis' *Who's Who in America*. Mr. Long has written and will shortly publish memoirs of his life and career.

www.ingramcontent.com/pod-product-compliance
Lightning Source LLC
Chambersburg PA
CBHW050526190326
41458CB00045B/6725/J